INTRODUCTION

I was recently at our family ranch with friends and they started asking me questions about the place and about my family. As they prodded me to tell story after story, some historical and some funny, many about the Ranch since that is where we were at the time, I realized how much there was to tell! That is where this "book", or series of stories with family history is originating. It finally dawned on me that our history is too rich and abundant not to share with future generations. Some of this is historical, but along the way there were some interesting and funny true stories that should be kept alive.

I must give a special thank you to my sister, Valerie Hale Gillum, for helping me with the research and proofing of this book. She was a tremendous help and devoted many hours to assisting me! I also, want to thank Thomas Powers, my second cousin, for collaborating with me on research. He assisted me more than I assisted him, but we did exchange family history, documents, letters, pictures, and stories while he was writing a book on his father, Joshua Bryant Powers. He is still writing it at this time, but it will be titled, "Perfect Heaven, My Father's American Life." A big thank you to my son, Byron Hale Werner, for hours of formatting the pictures and page layouts, and helping me publish this book. And, last but certainly not least, I have to thank Kelly Hoffman Davis and her mother, Kathy Hoffman for planting the seed at the Ranch that spurred me into action.

My husband, Jack, and I collect a lot of Sioux or Plains Indian artifacts, art, and décor and have admired that race. We have a great deal of admiration for the American Indians. They passed stories down from generation to generation. And, we have done that too, but as the family grows some of those stories are bound to be lost, not to mention the new stories I learned during the research for this book. If it ends here, just the retelling of stories, then I will be happy. If something else comes of this, well, that remains to be seen.

Housekeeping Detail: The names and dates that are in bold are because those are direct ancestors or descendants. Others are mentioned but not in bold because they are not descendants of the Powers or Hale families. Also, my grandchildren's ancestors are also highlighted, as are my adopted nieces.

PART I

HALE/POWERS HISTORY

CHAPTER I
POWERS FAMILY ANCESTORS

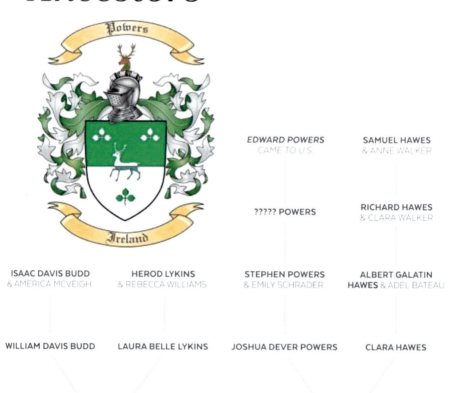

Le Poer, de la Poer, Powyr, Power, Powers are all variants of the same name. The "s" was added when they came to America. In 1066, one of the knights of William's train was a LePoer. The family were proprietors of large estates in Great Britain and were considered landed gentry. Robert or Roger LePoer was a knight who went to Ireland with Henry II (1133-1189). He received large land grants from the crown for his distinguished service. The LePoer family settled in County Down and Waterford and became renowned as an influential and warlike race. They remained the most powerful and numerous of families in Waterford until the first half of the 20th century. Queen Elizabeth I, (1558-1603, reign) made the family leader the Earl of Tyrone. He had no sons, and his estate passed into the hands of English heirs. Queen Elizabeth's knight and master of the horses was Sir Henry Power. But, the Powers were known as tried and true warriors.

During the reign of Edward III (1327-1377 reign) there were nine Barons with the Power name. Sir Henry Power, the son, was commander of the army in Ireland in 1620. In 1750 Lady Catherine Power married James O'Brian.

Edward Powers of Ireland was shipped to the US in a hogshead because he was rebellious. He was the great grandfather of Stephan Powers. His brothers were John, Snowden, Evans and Hiram. Hiram was the father of the famous sculptor, Hiram Powers.

Stephen Powers (1820-1902)

Stephen, each spring, would build a long log raft in Ohio and fill the cabin on top with merchandise, he would then sell his wares along the river to New Orleans. He would finally sell the logs and make his way back up the Natchez Trace to Ohio to prepare for another spring, and repeat the process. One year, he got as far as Hawesville, Kentucky where he tied up, and let his dog off the raft. His dog was attacked by a big red rooster and a dog-rooster fight developed. The dog won, the rooster died, and my great great grandfather was thrown in jail. There he stayed until the water receded, so there was nothing for him to do but set up shop right there in Hawesville.

***

Emily Shrader Powers (1829-1858)

He married Emily Shrader (1829-1858). She gave birth to Joshua, but died very young. Stephen then married Susan. She was described by her stepson, Joshua Dever Powers as "a quick-moving, fun-loving, piano-playing, tiny great lady who spent her years in a doll house high on a hill. Grand—mammy brought Stephen's younger children into the world and brought up Joshua, a mildly Protestant boy who stole an ardent Clara (Hawes) from her Catholic upbringing." Stephen brought up two families in Hawesville, had a store in a nice brick building called the Powers Block, and left it to Joe Sapp. He met Joe on a cold morning when Stephen came upon Joe outside his store, ice cold blue legs and all. He took the frightened boy into the store and put warm stockings and shoes on him. Joe never left Stephen, working for him his whole life and then owning the store when Stephen died at the age of 82 on 1902.

***

Joshua Dever "J. D." Powers (1844-1923)

Col. JD Powers was born in Hawesville, Kentucky on October 17, 1844. At the age of twenty-one he met Clara Hawes and fell madly in love. She fled a convent in Hawesville and eloped with Joshua. She was seventeen and he was twenty-three. Clara had a senator in her family, and her grandmother was a great French lady who had fled from slave labor riots on one of the West Indian sugar growing islands. Clara was a force to be reckoned with; a cane wielding, elegant, spendthrift, who when breaking something in a store would remark, "Oh. Just charge it to the Colonel!"

***

Hawes Genealogy:
Samuel Hawes – Unknown history

Samuel Hawes II – m.(married) Anne Walker of Caroline County Virginia. Both came from prominent land holding families.

Richard Hawes – m. Clara Walker in 1792 in Caroline County. They lived there for eighteen years, and had eight children. He moved to Kentucky in 1810, first Jefferson County, then in 1819 to Daviess County. In 1820, they purchased 3,000 acres from Iceland Landing, ten miles above Owensburg on the Ohio River to the hills of Yelvington. He acquired a large tract of land in Hancock Co. A few years later he donated this land and on January 3, 1829, Hawesville became a town named after him.

***

Clara Hawes Powers (1848-1915)

Another Clara Hawes story as told by my mother (Lucille) to my second cousin, Thomas Powers and hand recorded in his diary in 1972:

"But above all Clara was an imperious woman. She had working for her an old colored woman. One day the old woman's granddaughter came by the house, a buxom, high-spirited fifteen-year-old, and Clara fancied that she had been sassed. "Don't you sass me, girl," said Clara, out watering the flowers with a garden hose in Louisville. "What would your grandmother say?" "You come here. Why, Lord, girl, you smell, you stink. Don't you ever take a bath"? You ought to be ashamed of yourself, dressed like that, smelling like that." She grabbed the girl by the arm and shoved the garden hose down the front of her dress. "Your grandma's a decent woman, and look at you!" Then she called the servants of the house. "Take this girl inside and scrub her and get her some decent clothes." The servants, Lucille said, hated to do it but followed orders. They scrubbed the girl from top to toe and then gave her clean clothes from Clara's own dresser – underwear, dress, petticoats. "Now your Grandma doesn't have to be ashamed of you. Get along!""

JD and Clara

J. D. was admitted to the Kentucky bar. He later moved to Owensboro, Kentucky where he practiced law and conducted a small bank. He moved to Louisville about 1892 to organize the United States Trust Co. JD was also a 32nd degree Mason. He was appointed by President Cleveland to the position of "collector of internal revenue" from 1895 to 1899.

The title of Colonel was given to him by early acquaintances and friends. There is no indication he served in the military. He was the founder of Commonwealth Life Insurance Co. and a prominent citizen of Louisville, Kentucky financial circles. He was a successful corporate lawyer and founded the United States Trust Company in 1903 and served as its president for two years. He also served a term as president of the American Banker's Association in 1907.

J. D.'s wife, Clara Hawes died in 1915. They had seven sons and two daughters: the sons were Stephen Powers 1866-1944) of Las Vegas, Albert Douglas, "A. D." Powers (1868-1945) of St. Petersburg, FL, Col. Robert Boyd Powers (US Army retired) (1871-1941) Owensboro, KT, Joshua Dever Powers (1876-1956) Whitesvillage, New York City. Jay Clay Powers, my grandfather, (1880-1922) predeceased his father by a year. John H. Powers (1882-?) of New York City. JD's daughters were Jessie C. Powers (????-????), Owensboro and Emily Hawes Powers (1884-?), Indianapolis, and then the west coast, and finally, Thomas Powers (1890-1955). J.D. Powers died of apoplexy following a lengthly illness from strokes in 1923. We should note here that his son, my grandfather, was murdered the previous year which more than likely took a toll on his failing health, as well. He was a very well respected man. And, he adored my mother. In his later years, he was estranged from many of his children and grandchildren.

This was written to my cousin Thomas Powers from Lucille, my mother, in a letter about her grandfather, Joshua Dever:

"I looked forward to my visits to him and he would be waiting by the station, and I would race from the train and leap into his arms. He would carry me and introduce me to everyone – black and white – as his dear little granddaughter. He regretted not knowing his children better, and well realized in his old age the mistakes he had made. I firmly believe that grandma was greatly responsible. She spoiled them one minute and whipped them the next, but always preached at them and threatened them about 'Your father!' She instilled an almost Godly fear of him. "

He had a great quote referring to Lucille's sister, Clara Hawes (named after her grandmother) when Clara II was being smart with him. JD said, "Don't worry, Lena, my grandmother, it's just the sap beginning to rise." Since JD was estranged from his children, I don't know what happened to his wealth. It certainly was not passed down to his favorite granddaughter. This is from his company's tribute to him at a memorial service.

The following Expression of Appreciation
Of the service of
Col. J. D. Powers
Was unanimously adopted at the Nineteenth Annual Meeting
of the Stockholders of the Commonwealth Life
Insurance Company, held Wednesday,
February 14, 1923

Colonel J. D. Powers, the Chairman of the Board of Directors of this Company, died quite suddenly about 5pm January 31, 1923. While he had been an invalid for the past two years and had been unable to be at the office since the Fall of 1921, still the end came unexpectedly as we had all hoped that he would be spared for some time to come.

Colonel Powers was elected president of this Company at the first meeting of the board of directors in February, 1905, and served continuously in that position until February, 1922, when on account of his failing health, he asked to be relieved of the duties of President and he was thereupon elected Chairman of the Board, which position he held at the time of his death.

Col. Powers was a man of sterling integrity, fine business judgement and high character, and we, the Stockholders of the Company, feel that in his death we have lost a most efficient and capable officer and one who contributed in no small measure to the success and prosperity of the Company. We tender our sincere sympathy to his family in their bereavement and we direct that this appreciation of the services of Colonel Powers be spread on the minutes and that a copy be sent to each one of his children and to each stockholder in this Company.

Jay Clay Powers (1880-1922)

Jay wanted to be a playwright, but studied law at Leland Stanford University instead. He did write several plays, some of which can be found on the internet. "Sam Bo-jam, and His African Colony: A Negro Farce in Three Scenes", 1916, "A Day in Court: A Burlesque on a Justice of the Peace's Court", 1915, "If I Only Had a Million: A Comedy in Three Acts", "Elsie in Dreamland: A Fantastical Play for Children", 1915 and "Money in the Movies: A Husky Dusky Mellow—dramer", 1917. And to our surprise we found them on Amazon!

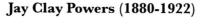

Lena Laird Budd (1880-1932)

Jay married Lena Laird Budd (1880-1932) in 1903. Lena was born in Charleston West Virginia.

***

Issac Davis Budd(????-????)
America McVeigh (1831-?)

Lena's grandparents were Issac Davis Budd (unknown) and America McVeigh.

***

William Davis Budd (1854-1919)
Laura Belle Lykins Budd ((1837-1882)

Lena's parents were William Davis Budd (1854-1919) and Laura Belle Lykins. Lena and Jay's first daughter, **Clara Hawes Powers (1904-1917)**, was born nine months and four days later. He later found out that his father planned to send him to law school, but he eloped with Lena, and JD never made the offer. He pursued his play writing but eventually enrolled in Leland Stanford University to study law, presumably paying for his own education.

***

Lucille Powers Hale (1911-1981)

My mother, **Laura Lucille Powers (1911-1981**) was a child of about three or four while he was attending Stanford. Clara was devoted to her baby sister, Lucille,

Lucille

Lucille and Lena

but she died during an appendix operation and was buried on her thirteenth birthday. Lucille, also came down with appendicitis when she was thirteen and was scared to death she would also die. Obviously, her surgery was a success. Clara Hawes (I) doted on her namesake granddaughter, but after Little Clara died, she had no use for her other grandchildren, including my mother. As previously stated, Joshua Dever adored Lucille and she him. She always looked forward to visiting him and he would take her around introducing her to his friends and then sit her on his lap.

***

Jay Clay became a Major in the US Army and during World War I was stationed in Paris, France. My grandmother and mother moved from San Antonio to Chicago because Lena could make a better wage teaching, and the cost of living was lower. She describes living in an apartment and having to do the cleaning herself. Lucille had a victory garden across the street in a vacant lot with the other children from the apartment building. While Jay Clay was stationed in Paris, and practicing law for the Army, Lt. Conrad Hilton (founder of the

Major Powers and driver

13

1918 Major Jay Clay Powers

Hilton Hotel chain) was his adjutant. They became very good friends during this time, often dining together at the officer's mess and going to restaurants when they could. During the war, they decided they would go into business together, the hotel business. When they came back to the states, they settled in Texas and started their hotel partnership. They bought up old hotels, with mostly Connie's money from his mother, and set about modernizing and redecorating them. The first hotel was the Melba Hotel in Cisco, Texas, the second, the Mobley Hotel in Fort Worth, and then the Waldorf in Dallas. For the Waldorf, they needed additional capital and took on a third partner, David C. Soderman, a man they didn't really know. They also didn't know he had been arrested in El Paso and his sanity had been tested two weeks prior to what seemed like a normal Tuesday morning.

Jay and unknown soldier

On that fateful day, April 18, 1922, my mother, Laura Lucille, aged ten, was playing with her dolls on the floor of their hotel suite. When Jay came to kiss her good-bye before leaving to attend a company picnic, she was too busy playing with her dolls and wouldn't give him a kiss. Jay left via the elevator to the lobby of the hotel. My grandmother, Lena, received a call from the lobby telling her to come quick. Soderman had shot Jay Clay right through the upper abdomen. Jay fell, and Soderman fired a second shot into his stomach. An off-duty detective grabbed Soderman before he

could empty the pistol into my grandfather. This was just a few blocks over from where many years later John F. Kennedy would be assassinated in 1960. Jay Clay was taken to the hospital and lived less than two hours before he succumbed to his wounds.

There are various theories as to why Soderman murdered Jay Clay. One is that he was in love with my grandmother and jealous of Jay's beautiful wife and little girl. Another, was that he and his wife (Ethel) had a fight and she left him, a third theory was that Jay was having an affair with Ethel. That theory didn't ring true because Jay had stated on several occasions that he didn't like the woman and didn't want to be around her. My mother remembers Soderman telling her how pretty she was and that he wished he had a little girl just like her. My grandmother and mother testified at the trial as to Jays whereabouts on certain dates that proved he had never been in the company of Mrs. Soderman privately. But the charges were reduced from first degree murder to manslaughter and Soderman was sentenced to five years, but after three his family bought a pardon from Governor Ma Ferguson. He started drinking again after his release and died within the year.

Joshua Bryant Powers

***

Joshua Bryant Powers (1892- 1989)

(Powers Family Story, by Joshua Bryant Powers (Lucille's first cousin, his father was Albert (AD) Powers, Jay Clay's brother)

Joshua was born on August 25, 1892 in a village called Habit, Kentucky. His mother was having trouble progressing in labor so Dr. McWhorter, threatened to "Quill" her. They would take a goose quill, fill it with snuff, and blow it up the expectant mother's nose. It would cause such a sneezing fit that the labor process was usually thrown into action. His mother went into labor before the doctor had to administer "the quill", the threat alone did the trick.

Joshua was my mother's favorite cousin and he came to visit us often. We also visited them at their Pelham Manor home in New York City. Joshua worked for United Press Association, much of his life in Buenos Aires, Argentina and other South American countries. He had a firm, Joshua B. Powers, Inc. that represented newspapers in foreign countries. He won many coveted awards for his writing and nonprofit philanthropic efforts. I remember as a child getting a turtle pin with emerald like eyes. I loved that pin and had it well into my adulthood. I went to find it when I started writing this book and couldn't. He belonged to a society that worked effortlessly to save the turtles in the Caribbean. He was known as the man who saved the sea turtles. I have many fond memories of "Uncle Bryant". For more information on him, see the book that his son and author, Thomas Powers, is writing as I write this, "Perfect Heaven, My Father's American Life." It is sure to be a wonderful book.

Joshua Bryant Powers married Susan Moore Powers (1908-1974). They had four children: Caroline Hayes White Powers (1926-2009), known as Chica, Joshua B. Powers Jr. (1938-), known as Bushrod, Thomas Moore Powers (1940-), the author, and Susan Hopkinson Powers Urstadt (1942-1997). Susan, being the same age as my sisters visited us a couple of times and spent a week with us at the Ranch. Tom sent me this information that is not directly related to us because it is his mother's side, but I love this stuff, so have I to include it. This was his response when I asked what his middle name was.

"My middle name is Moore — my mother named me after her father, who was named David Thomas Moore, but never used or was known as David — always called Tom, and called DTM by his three daughters when speaking of him. He was not at all pleased to have a grandson named after him and told my mother he would have much preferred her to name me Francis Hopkinson Smith Powers after his uncle, the painter and novelist F. Hopkinson Smith, who designed the base of the statue of liberty and many lighthouses on the East Coast — Marine architect was his first profession — sold more novels than you can believe, was one of the speakers at Mark Twain's 75th birthday party in NYC — very interesting guy."

CHAPTER 2
TOM POWERS, THE ACTOR

Tom Powers (1890-1955)

Tom Powers was a famous movie (80 films) and stage actor. Jay Clay's brother. *These stories mostly come from Thomas Powers, Pulitzer Prize winning author and son of Joshua Bryant Powers, grandson of A. D. Powers. Some of these stories were told to him by my mother, Lucille Powers on a trip to his farm in Vermont in 1977. He recorded them in his diary. Here Tom will refer to the actor, Thomas will refer to the author.*

"Tom was the seventh son born on the seventh day of the seventh month... He always used to say, 'I had a sister fat, and I had a sister Lena.'" [One of his sisters was fat, and he had a sister-in-law named Lena – i.e., Lena Budd, Lucille's mother.] Told by Joshua Bryant Powers to his son Thomas, the author, my second cousin. Thomas was named after his great uncle, the actor.

Joshua Bryant Powers, (Lucille's first cousin and favorite cousin), and Lucille both agreed that Tom Powers was a sadist, a man with a capacity for deliberate cruelty. After the murder of her father, Lucille and her mother went to Louisville to stay with Joshua Dever Powers (Jay Clay's father, Lucille's grandfather). Tom, at the time, was already an established actor – thirty-two years old in 1922, at the height of his career – and Lucille, who dreamt secretly of the stage, was in breathless awe of her handsome uncle. She was just about eleven years old. One day she went out for a walk with Tom and another girl Lucille's age. The other girl took Tom's right hand. Lucille, excited, proud, half in love, reached for his left.

"Don't do that!" he snapped, stopping, turning on her. Lucille backed away, thought she would faint.

"But she's holding your hand," said Lucille.

"Yes," said Tom in a cold voice, "but she's a special friend of mine."

Lucille turned and ran all the way back to the house, managing to restrain her tears till she was inside the door.

"Years later I told Tom how much he hurt me and he apologized and seemed very upset," said Lucille. "I don't think he knew how it hurt me at the time."

"Yes, he did," said Joshua Bryant. "He was a sadist. He specialized in hurting people."

"But he could be so nice and charming!" said Lucille.

"When he wanted to be. He could walk into a party and take it over. He could charm everybody in the room. But, generally, it was all directed at somebody in the room, and he ruined everything for that one person. That was his specialty."

Thomas Powers wrote, "I started by writing that Father and Lucille agreed Tom was a sadist. They didn't. It pained Lucille to think so. She would admit he could be cruel, but not that he was a sadist. [Diary, 7 July 1977.]

1906. Tom Powers at 16 is enrolled at the American Academy of Dramatic Arts in New York, financed by his father, Joshua Dever. [Joshua Bryant Powers, referred here as JBP, plus New York Times, 10 November 1955.]

August 1914. "At the outbreak of World War One, Tom was in England making a movie of Barnaby Ridge [released in 1915] – he played the title character. He was also in a play called "Oh Joy!" in England but "Oh Boy!" when it came to New York. [JBP]

February 1917. Tom Powers opened as George Budd in Jerome Kern's Oh Boy! in New York on 20 February 1917 and ran 463 performances. He remained in the role when the musical moved to London, where it was re-named Oh Joy! In January 1919.

1917. "Oh Boy! Is worth every cent of the price. The piece is clean as a whistle and bright and keen of wit as Damascus steel… The young fellow is Tom Powers, whom we have seen twice already in this season in straight shows – Mr. Lazarus and Mile-a-Minute Kendall. All young Powers' cleverness couldn't save either from being failures, and I'm glad to see him in a hit at last, even if he had to go into a fresh realm, that of musical, to achieve it." "Here's hoping Tom Powers comes safe back to us from France! He's a fine boy with a versatile talent. Besides acting and songwriting, he has inherited some of the gift for modeling that made his ancestor Hiram Powers, a famous sculptor, and he has drawn magazine covers which have actually been displayed on newsstands." [Matthew White Jr., "The Stage," Munsey's Magazine, May 1917.]

18 March 1918. "Tom Powers, who won considerable popularity in New York last season for his natural performances in "Mr. Lazarus" and "Oh Boy," was a visitor to Broadway last week. He is a member of the Royal Flying Corps and is on his way to Europe, following a course of training in Montreal and Texas." [The Dramatic Mirror, 30 March 1918.]

Murial Brassler and Tom Powers, "Julius Caesar"

In England, he trained pilots during the war, crashed, and came back to the U.S. after he recovered. "He was based in Scotland during the war where he was an inspector over five divisions – met with a serious accident while on duty, his plane collapsing at a height of 700 feet;" spent nearly a year recovering in a London infirmary. [Wm. Connelly, et. al., History of Kentucky, vol. 4, 1922.]   Tom described his war in a book of poems, Flights (Macy-Masius), published in November 1926, which tells the story of his experience as a flyer in the Great War, from Camp Everman, Texas, where he was trained by the British Royal Flying Corps, thru his extended stay in two hospitals – Creigleith Hospital in Edinburgh, Scotland; and Cliveden Hospital in Buckinghamshire. He had lived by a fluke – he forgot to fasten his seat belt and was thrown out after the first bump; the second drove the engine through the pilot's seat where Tom would have been strapped in tight. At Creigleith he wrote, "I've been here three days now, with a broken nose, a twisted neck, two broken ankles, a dislocated shoulder... My nose is very swollen and my eyes are purple and blue and green; and my head, where I was knocked out, feels like God knows what." The docs had to re-break his ankles and warned him he might never walk again, but he did.

"Powers... appeared in over 70 silent films from 1911 to 1917... [and later in] such productions as Eugene O'Neill's Strange Interlude (1927)." Became a full time film actor after his role in Billy Wilder's film noir classic Double Indemnity (1944) and appeared thereafter in 80 films and television roles "usually playing middle-aged business men, military or police officers." But don't forget Destination Moon [1950] and Julius Caesar [1953]. [Wikipedia.]

7 September 1919. Tom married Meta Murray Janney Powers (1898-1983) in Philadelphia, where her father bought a house on Chestnut Hill (37 Summit Street) the following year. Meta had a twin sister – Alice Janney Grannis – and sometime after Tom died in 1955, Meta and Alice lived together in Manhattan Beach, where both died – Alice in 1980, Meta on 26 September 1983. [Marriage reported in the New York Times, 8 September 1929.]

1928-1929. Tom opened as Charles Marsden in Eugene O'Neil's Strange Interlude, his longest run in a Broadway play. [New York Times, 10 November 1955.]

24 September 1931. Tom opened as the title character in He, a comedy by Alfred Savoir; with Claude Rains and Violet Kemble Cooper. Stark Young in The New Republic, 7 Oct 31, was lukewarm: "Among the actors nobody except Claude Rains seemed aware of the philosophical hints of the speeches. Mr. Rains as the Napoleonic egoist knew what he meant. The rest of the company played away blindly with their several methods." It ran for 40 performances. A cartoon of the three principals by Hirschfeld appeared in the NY Herald Tribune on 27 Sept 31.

1931. Tom published a second book of poems about the First World War, The Span (Molliston Company).

February 1932. Tom Powers stared in his own play, Handy Man, when it opens at the Copley Theater in Boston in February. The Harvard Crimson's "R.O.B." liked it: "The versatile Tom Powers outdoes his justly famous efforts in [Shaw's] The Apple Cart and Strange Interlude… Sophistication takes a well-earned evening's rest. The blasé affections of the socially ambitious are held up to the scorching ridicule of Mr. Powers' homely eloquence until they are babbled to cringing subjection by his irrepressible tongue, reinforced with frequent inhibitions of well-spiked punch." The play was published by Samuel French in 1939.

13 March 1932. Tom Powers opened in The First Fifty Years by Henry Myers at the Princess Theater in New York; it runs for 48 performances, closing at the end of April.

1934. Tom published his first novel, A Scotch Circus (Houghton Mifflin).

1935. Johnson Wax of Racine, Wisconsin began "experimenting with Radio Sponsorship to advertise their products. The best-known result of this experiment is the long running, much beloved series Fibber McGee and Molly which would be a regular feature on NBC until 1959. Another lesser known, but well done effort, is the quarter hour program with actor Tom Powers called Life Studies. Powers had dedicated his life to the Broadway stage, but took time to appear in 70 silent films between 1911 and 1917. From 1916 to 1944 he enjoyed great success as a playwright, actor and director. He returned to the silver screen at the invitation of Billy Wilder to appear in the noir classic, Double Indemnity. He would appear in over 80 films. The Life Studies programs featured Powers as the sole player. After an intro by announcer Howard Claney (who would get several opportunities to plug

Johnson wax products during the 1 minute, but never as artfully as Fibber McGee's Harlow Wilcox) Powers would give a short introduction to the night's story. Powers usually added some poetry to the introduction. Powers published his stories in a pair of books, Life Studies and More Life Studies, in 1939 and 1945." [Old Time Radio Catalog.]

1941. Walter Kerr: "In 1941 a supreme effort was made to [introduce American audiences to Chekhov]... Katherine Cornell, Judith Anderson, Ruth Gordon, Dennis King, Edmund Gwenn, Tom Powers and Alexander Knox joined forces to produce The Three Sisters. At least four of these people were independent stars... [but] they could do no more than eke out a thinnish run in New York and a few disappointing weeks on the road." [Walter Kerr, How Not to Write a Play, p. 20]

1948-1950. Tom Powers took over the role of the father in Columbia Pictures' series about a dog in the Lassie mode, beginning with For the Love of Rusty (1948). Last film in the series was Rusty's Birthday (1950). [Armstrong, Encyclopedia of Film Themes, p. 174]

1946. Tom published a third novel, Sheba on Trampled Grass (Bobbs Merrill).

1948. Tom Powers played an army post commander opposite Agnes Moorehead in a Dick Powell-Jane Greer western, Station West.

9 November 1955. Tom dies at his home in Manhattan Beach, California, "after a long illness." [New York Times, 10 November 1955.]

22 November 1966. Joshua Bryant Powers letter to Lucille Hale, about a tea set that Tom Powers' widow hoped to sell, suggesting that Lucille buy it for one of her daughters, or, if they are uninterested, letting JBP buy it for one of his: "I do remember Tom speaking about it and saying that he wished that it would remain in the hands of one of the family…Meta probably needs the money, and I would not quibble about the price." Not sure what happened to the tea set.

CHAPTER 3
LUCILLE

Lucille, "The Mascot", at Stanford while her father was studying law.

Laura Lucille Powers Hale (1911-1981)

Laura Lucille was born in San Antonio, Texas. She went by the name of Lucille. My mother remembered riding her tricycle though the arcade at Stanford University when my grandfather, Jay Clay, was studying law. Little did she know that in 1938 she would wed my father in that very chapel she rode her bike around. After Lucille's father was murdered, they went to live with Joshua Dever for a time and her mother, my grandmother, Lena Lykins Budd Powers, began to teach. Lena eventually taught at Boston College, the first female to do so., I was told. They took many road trips (see Lucille and Lena). On one such road trip to California Lucille was in Yosemite National Park when a man commented that she should be in Hollywood. They moved to Los Angeles for Lucille to pursue an acting career. (More on this below).

After my mother married my father she had four children. Loralyn (1941), Valerie (1943), Marsha (1944), and then the "postscript", Charise (1952). Lucille was active in local theater companies and did several plays, two notable ones were "A Streetcar Named Desire" and "The "Barrett's of Whimpole Street." She was a brilliant actress and got rave reviews for every role she played. She was also a member of Peninsula Children's Theater Association from 1953 to her death in 1981. She did many plays and excelled as the witch in the "Wizard of Oz." She was so good that all my friends were frightened of her for weeks after the play! Her acting skills allowed her to mesmerize audiences with readings where she would read all the parts, changing her voice and mannerisms so you forgot it was just one person performing.

She was also active in the Red Cross during WWII, active in St. Paul's Episcopal Church, at our schools, and was a Girl Scout leader for each of us.

Conrad Nicholson Hilton (1887-1979)

Connie and Lucille

Conrad Hilton remained close to my grandmother and mother. When my mother was leaving Los Angeles to travel to San Francisco to marry my father in 1938, she stayed at Connie's Bel Air home and he said, "Don't go, Monk, (he always called her Monk, as her father did, because her father thought she looked like a monkey when she was born) stay here and marry me instead." But, of course, my mother was in love with my father and left for San Francisco, though touched by his kindness. Connie was Catholic, and a deeply religious man.

In many ways, he was a simple and naïve man, I came to discover. Obviously, not in business. His estate included 8 acres and backed up to 6 holes of the Bel Air golf course. The previous owner had a 1000 square foot building that was a dog kennel.

At the time of this writing, it is for sale for $225m. The woman hung original Monet's and Renoir's to brighten the dog's moods! The main house had a full-sized hotel elevator, a regular kitchen, and a "smelly" kitchen for foods like fish. There were spacious living rooms, a library, two dining rooms, servants quarters and several bedrooms upstairs (five, I think). The bedrooms were enormous, and ZsaZsa Gabor (Hilton) had a bedroom all in pink satin. No one ever slept in that bedroom after they were divorced. He told my mother that he didn't sleep with ZsaZsa until they were married. I am sure that was a first for her! And, he hadn't slept with her for 10 months prior to her becoming pregnant with Francesca Hilton, but since they were still legally married, he was a gentleman if nothing else, he gave Francesca his name. There was a beautiful pool with a guest house the size of a lot of people's main houses. In Connie's later years he married Francis, a longtime friend and lovely woman. She was so good to Connie and they made a great couple. She and my mother became great friends. My mother and I visited often and Connie came to San Francisco frequently.

Lena and Lucille, c. 1931

***

After my grandfather was killed, my grandmother, Lena Budd Powers, went back to school, got her Master's degree and became a professor at Boston College. She taught English and Drama. Every summer my mother and grandmother would take a road trip. Two women in the 1920s in a car traveling by themselves, changing tires, stopping for meals, staying in hotels. That had to be highly unusual. Here my grandmother describes a trip in a letter to her sister-in-law Mabel (A.D. Power's second wife).

"I worked hard as it is possible for one to work until the second week in August, then we got into the Ford and started off, Lucille, the dog, and I. We had a wonderful trip, 2400 miles all together, and not a flat tire the whole trip. I can almost say we came home on Boston air. We went to New York, down through Philadelphia, Baltimore, Washington, to Richmond, where we stayed with my folks for two weeks, then back across Virginia to Staunton, up the Shenandoah Valley, visiting Endless Caverns, and Luray Cave, through Harper's Ferry, Frederic, Maryland, Gettysburg, Harrisburg, Williamsport, to Watkin's Glen, New York, a wonderful place, then to Niagra, back across New York, down the Lebanon Trail to Pittsfield Mass., over Jacob's Ladder, and home. A wonderful scenic trip, every bit of it."

Portfolio Head Shot

Texas Bad Man, 1932

This was in 1924. I don't know about you, but I'm impressed! They went to

Florida, the Carolinas, Kentucky, and finally to California in 1926 after my mother graduated from high school at the age of 15.

While in Yosemite, my mother was told she should go to Hollywood and be in the movies. So, they ventured down to Los Angeles, my mother did film tests and was hired as a contract player with Warner Bros. She did a screen test with Douglas Fairbanks, Sr., and he told her she was a real actress and that he felt everything she did. However, she did not get that part for he was very short, 5'6", and my mother was too tall, 5'8", for him. They wanted a girl who was two inches shorter than my mother. He was very disappointed and thought they could overcome that. The studio disagreed. As a matter of fact, this was a common problem in Hollywood, and they would make doorways for the men and another for the women. They would look to be the same door, but the doorway was much lower and narrower for the man to make him appear to be taller and broader than the female when she stood in the "same" door.

It was after this screen test that she was given a contract. She writes to her Aunt Mabel, that "Doug (Douglas Fairbanks) and Mary (Mary Pickford) are sure sweet! Tell Uncle A.D. that his favorite actress (Mary Pickford) is just as lovely in person as on the screen!" She starred with Tom Mix, Ken Maynard, Phillip Holmes and Adolf Menjou. Mr. Menjou bought her a winter coat while filming "Man To Man" back east because she was freezing to death in her California one. She said he was a very nice man, much older, but expected nothing in return. Yes, the casting couch was alive and plentiful even in the early years of movies. She was an excellent actress, and I wonder now if she didn't refuse some of those

Advertising "Billy the Kid"

"casting couch" offers, because she was the female lead in the earlier films, but not in the later ones. Her acting is far superior than some of her costars that overacted terribly due to previously being in silent films.

Lucille never did silent films. Her movies were "Three Weekends" with Clara Bow (1928), "Man to Man" (1931), "Two Gun Man" (1931), "Amateur Daddy" (1931), "Texas Bad Man" (1932), "Only Yesterday" (1933), and "The Mystic Hour" (1934).

Phillip Holmes and Lucille Powers "Barber John's Boy"

My mom was friends with many of the stars of that day like Joan Crawford. Cary Grant asked her for a date, but she turned him down to go out with my father. Not a bad choice since my father had the same build, blue eyes, and was very handsome. When hearing this story, I exclaimed, "Cary Grant could have been my father!" The Three Stooges used to pass her on the lot and all bow at the same time, 'Saying, Good Morning, Miss Powers."

When my mother turned 18 they had a birthday party on the set and my grandmother exclaimed, "Lucille, you are finally 18!" Everyone was shocked into silence since it was the law that she should be tutored on the set until she was eighteen and had never been tutored since starting at Warner Bros. My grandmother didn't think it was necessary since she had already graduated high school at 15. They had lied about her age for three years, so everyone thought she was turning 21!

They lived in a bungalow in Beverly Hills, but money was very tight. They would wrap nylons separately at Christmas to make more presents for each other. When my mother was 21 her mother got breast cancer. She battled it for months and suffered

Hear no evil, see no evil, speak no evil, a modeling photo

terribly, finally she refused all food, when that didn't work, she refused all water. She knew my mother couldn't keep up with the endless bills, and she knew she was terminal. This was 1932. The morphine was feeding her body and she had had enough. She passed away about 8 days after refusing all water, and my mother had her "laid out" in the dining room. This sounds horrible to us today, but it was the custom in those days. My mother always said it was quite soothing for her to have her there for a couple more days.

Publicity shot

CHAPTER 4
HALE FAMILY ANCESTORS

HALE FAMILY
Ancestors

HALE FAMILY
Genealogy:

Starting with this author's Great, great, great, great, great, great, great, great grandfather:

Thomas Hale - was the second of five children, and only son of **Thomas and Joan Kirby** (dates unknown). *

***

Thomas Hale -born here is signified by "b." in Watton Herfordshire, England **(6/15/1606-12/21/1682)** Married here it is signified by "m." **Thomasine Dewsett (??-1/30/1682)**. M. 12/11/1632 at St. Helen's Bishopgate, London. Came to America, Newbury, MA in 1635. Thomas buried in Newbury, MA. He was appointed to try cases and was Constable in 1649. He was one of the first Selectmen chosen in Haverhill in 1646. *

***

Thomas Hale (II) - b. Newbury, MA **(11/18/1633-10/22/1688)** M. **Mary Hutchinson (12/28/1630-12/8/1715)** M. on 5/26/1657. Buried Boxfield, MA. He was a fence-viewer, Selectman, trial juror, tything-man (elected official), highway surveyor, way-warden (takes care of the highway), and on committees of town. *

***

Joseph Hale - b. in Newbury, MA. **(2/20/1670-2/13/1761)** M. 11/15/1693 to **Mary Watson (??-2/1/1708)**. Joseph buried in Harvard, MA. Joseph was a Selectman and representative to the General Court and in early records called the Clerk of the bond. He was and ensign, lieutenant, and captain of the militia in 1728.*

***

Ambrose Hale - (7/16/1699-1/15/1767) m. **Hannah Symonds (4-13-1709-???)** M. on 12/10/1732 in Boxford, MA. He inherited 82 acres in Boxford from his father. Ambrose b. in Windhall, VT. *

Jacob Hale - (3/19/1769-11/14/1822) B. in Harvard, MA. Jacob was the eldest son of **Ambrose and Mercy**. M. **Roccina Beebe (???-1/12/1818)** in Windhall, VT in 1794 D. in Liverpool, NY. Became a teacher early in life.*

*Information derived from "Thomas Hale, 1637 Emigrant" by Louise G. Walker, c. 1978

***

Marshal Hale (I) (1809-1891)

Lineage: Jacob, Ambrose, Ambrose, Joseph, Thomas, Thomas, (this last Thomas came to Newberry, Mass in 1635)

For the Marshals, I will use Roman numerals after their names to help differentiate the three Marshals.

Marshal (I) was only nine when his mother died and thirteen when his father died. He was raised by relatives in Phoenix, New York that were too poor to provide an education. At twenty-one, he left home and became a day laborer in western New York. He then worked for a cooperage (making barrels) back in Phoenix, NY. He heard they were hiring laborers to construct the Oswega, Seneca, and Cayunga Canals in upper state New York. He had always wanted to own a store and this seemed like a good spot with all the workers needing goods. He worked on the canals as a day laborer and returned home to New York for the winter, and taking odd jobs, managed to save $100. In the spring of 1840, Marshal Hale journeyed to Syracuse and bought merchandise at a store called Dennis McCarthy. He returned to Lock # 1 on the Seneca Canal and opened a small store. The general merchandise store was successful from the beginning and he gained the reputation for honesty and friendliness.

The same year he married Carolyn Meech. They had a son, George Nathan in March of 1842. A few years later he got the news that other merchants were going to open stores near his. He knew he lacked skills in accounting and merchandising. So, he decided to go back to New York and learn better skills from his friends John Tomlison and E.T. Tefft, both successful merchants. While in New York, Marshal decided to get a haircut and shave. The barber took one look at his red fuzzy beard and said, "Put a little cream on that fuzz and let the cat lick it off!" The two merchants took him under their wing and taught him good accounting and ledger practices, took him to the wholesale houses, and taught him how to bargain shrewdly.

With renewed confidence, he returned to Lock #1, but soon learned of another merchant coming to open a store nearby. He proceeded for two full months to reduce one fourth of his merchandise to cost. Then he marked one fourth to only 10% above cost, marked another one fourth to 15% above cost, and the last fourth he sold at 20-25% above cost.

When the rival merchant opened his doors, the people soon realized the higher prices and returned to M. Hale Store for lower prices for the same goods. The competitor soon went out of business.

In 1846, James Marshal Hale was born and the store had become so prosperous that Marshal (I) opened two more. Eventually, he had established five stores in New York. Not content with just the stores, he invested in a cooperage and in his brother's ship building company. They built many of the boats that were seen on the canal. In November of 1849 his wife, Carolyn died, leaving the boys aged seven and three.

Two years later he married Clarissa Payne in 1851. She was devoted to the two small boys, but she died in 1852 after giving birth to Oliver Ambrose Hale. With two wives dying in such a short time, and now three boys to take care of, Marshal at the age of forty-three, sold his business interests and went to join his friend Evert Brown Dyckman in Schoolcraft, Michigan in 1853.

✳ ✳ ✳

Prudence Dyckman Cobb Hale (1828-1907)

Marshal met and married Evert's sister, Prudence Dyckman Cobb (1828-1907). Her first husband, Samuel Prentis Cobb passed away shortly after their daughter was born. She was a widow with a son, Frank Dyckman Cobb (1849) and a daughter, Carra Prentis Cobb (1852). In 1856 Marshal (I) and Prudence had a son, Evert William Hale, and another in 1858, Samuel Prentis Cobb Hale, named after Prudence's first husband. Marshal went into business with his father-in-law in South Haven, and through better practices, improved the lumbering and general merchandise company without putting in any of his $50,000 he brought from New York.

In 1860, Marshal wanted to leave Michigan and go to Chicago, however, the family objected to moving that far away from family. It is interesting that another young man did move to Chicago, Marshall Field, and many years after working for other retailers, opened his own store we all know as Marshall Field & Company. Marshal Hale opened a store of his own in Schoolcraft, and Prudence and Marshal moved into the house her parents had built for her and her first husband. Marshal brought with him the experience and expertise he had learned in his previous stores. He excelled and prospered in his store and the many other ventures in which both families were partners. The Hale boys literally grew up in the store. In 1861, Della

Gleason was born, in 1864, Jennie Eliza, in 1866, Marshal, Jr.(II) was born, and in 1869 their last child, Reuben Brooks arrived.

Marshal Hale (I) was having health trouble with the Michigan winters and was spending a good deal of the winter in Florida. He missed his family and decided to relocate his family to San Jose, California at the age of 64! At first, they were going to relocate to the East Bay, but Prudence's youngest sister, Harriet (married to D.D. Owens) lived in San Jose, and Prudence wanted to be closer to her. Marshal started putting up the money for the older boys to go into business and the younger ones were expected to keep the house and household ledger, see to the cows, chickens, and fruit trees, and even sell them at market. They had stores in San Jose, Salinas, Petaluma, Stockton and Sacramento. It was the first "chain" of stores in the state of California. Marshal Hale (I) died on June 15, 1891 one month before his 82nd birthday. He had suffered three strokes of apoplexy, the last occurring a few weeks before his death. The Rev. N. A. Haskel, pastor of the Unitarian Church said, "The great business ability and sterling integrity of the deceased made him an eminently successful man in all walks of life; and with all, he was ever so kindly to those with whom he came in contact." As the older boys started dying off, the three youngest sons started buying up the stores from their widows. The youngest three were Prentice Cobb, Marshal Hale II (1866-1945), and Reuben Brooks, forming Hale Bros. Department Stores, headquartered in San Francisco. Then their sons carried on the company, the three first cousins were Prentice Cobb II, and Marshal Hale III, or Marshal Hale, Jr. (1902-1989), and Newton, son of Reuben. Marshal was known as Marshal Jr. since his grandfather was already deceased. This was my father.

※※※

Dyckman Family History

This history was taken from an article entitled From Dyckman to Rich, origin unknown to this author.

For 239 years, land known as the "Dyckman Tract" remained in the hands of the Dyckman family. At its largest holdings, it included 400 acres in 1868 of what is now known as Manhattan, east of the Harlem River and west of Broadway. Dutchman, Jan Dyckman, founder of the land, arrived in America in 1660. He was fleeing Catholic persecution from Westphalia, County of Benthiem, Lower Saxony, Germany. The county was a state of the Holy Roman Empire. Because he was a prominent member of his new country, and a corporal of his military company during Indian troubles, the Dutch government awarded him a land track in 1677. He selected good soil parcels and rented many out to be farmed. One farm, for just one hen a year. Jan married Madeliene DeTourneur in 1673 and Rebecca Waldron in 1690. He died in 1715 leaving one child, Jacob, by Rebecca, born in 1692.

Jacob lived 81 years and married Jannette Kierson. He was a farmer experimenting with imported stock and seeds. He would not pay a toll to cross the Harlem River of one penny, so he and other farmers built their own "free" bridge which was known as the "Farmer's Bridge". Jacob had a son, William, born August 23,1725 and died August 10, 1787. William married the niece of Madeliene De Tourneur, Mary, who Anglicized her name to Turner. It should be mentioned here, that the land was not necessarily passed on to the eldest son, it was inherited by the son best suited to continue running the properties.

During the Revolutionary War the Dyckman land was occupied by the British army. William lived with a cousin in Peekskill. William's four sons all served their country, the colonies, during the Revolution. Jacobus was a soldier and later a member of the New York Constitutional Convention in 1821, he died in 1837. Michael was a lieutenant in the Westchester County Guides. Abraham (lieutenant) in the same unit, and his funeral was attended by George Washington. And, finally, William was a soldier at 13. When they returned to their land and home, the house had been burned by the British in retaliation to their service and support of the Colonists. The new house was built in 1783, on the same location as the old house. It is still there today, known as The Dyckman House. It is an old Dutch Farmhouse with a large veranda, massive chimneys and the "generous rooflines bespeak the homely comfort of the early Dutch settlers."

Jacobus' had two sons, Michael and Issac. They jointly inherited the estate. Isaac died in 1868, the last of the inheritors, leaving the estate to a nephew, son of Hannah Dyckman Smith, named Isaac Michael (1813-1899) who married the great granddaughter of Jacobus Dyckman. Her name was Fannie Blockwell Brown. I believe, they had no children and the estate was spread amongst nephews and nieces, and so broke up the 239-year holding of the Dyckman estate. The house is located at 204th Street and Broadway and is a historic museum to this day in New York City.

Hale / Dyckman Union

Back to William, who was the thirteen-year-old soldier. He married Maria Smith and had four children: William, Maria, Jane and Evert. Evert was born September 25, 1799 in Greenbush, New York. "He outlived four wives, three of them widows: Harriet Hinkley (married March 17, 1825, died February 17, 1938), they had nine children; Almire Hobbs Van Vranken (married October 16, 1839, died September 17, 1840) with two children, none with Evert); Amelia LeGrave Daniels (married September 9, 1841, died April 14, 1843) with two children and one more born after marrying Evert; and finally, Eliza Wood house Crossman (married November 25, 1844, date of death unknown), one child after marrying Evert." Evert fathered eleven children: Aaron, Prudence, Prudence II, Maria, Jane, Valentine, Esther, Isiah, Harriet, Jane II and Clovis. Evert Brown Dyckman was a cooper but also owned a dry good store and had a canal business nine miles north of Syracuse on the Oswego River. He needed some clothes and met his first wife, a seamstress, Harriet. She described him as a red-haired Irishman. They were married for twelve years and she died after the birth of their daughter, Harriet in 1893. That same year Evert moved with a large portion of his family in three wagons to Sinkbrook, Michigan. Young Harriet stayed behind with a family who could care for her at that time.

Evert, Prudence's father, married third wife, Amelia, paid off the mortgage to her house and added a wing to accommodate his large family. Evert was a business man and banker. He served in the state legislature in 1847, was the first president of Schoolcraft Village, Michigan in 1846, donated church steeples, and other civic improvements. He died in 1881 and was buried in Schoolcraft. Evert's third child, Prudence Tennant Dyckman, married twice. First to Samuel Prentis Cobb and then to Marshal Hale. (See info under Marshal Hale (1809-1891).

Interesting Anecdote: Harriet, the ninth child was raised by Mrs. DePuy, since her mother died in child birth and Mrs. DePuy had just lost a child and could therefore nurse her. Harriet was sent to boarding school and lived with a family name Owens. "When Mrs. Owens left on a visit, the Professor, her husband, and Harriet "found" each other. The shocked father, Evert, with "stern visage" and strong words ordered his errant daughter home. After a short time, Mrs. Owens visited Evert and persuaded him to let his daughter marry her husband. So, the professor got his divorce and a new wife." This is the same Harriet that would later move with Mr. Owens to San Jose, California.

Among the Dyckman heirs in the 1800s were doctors, lawyers, a Master of Arts, professional musicians, teachers, a surgeon, architect and builder, merchants, and bankers. Many attended the University of Michigan and a few the University of Chicago and quite a few of them were women, unusual for this time.

***

Marshal Hale II (1866-1945), born February 14th in Schoolcraft, MI, was seven when, in 1873, the family moved to California. He remembered seeing Prairie dogs and buffalo on his train trip across the country. In San Jose, Marshal (II) was charged with the ponies (Jack and Jim), chickens, and cows. He gathered lettuce from the garden and along with chicken eggs, took them to Chinatown to sell to the Chinese. Later, it was his job to collect the rent from the tenants and keep the ledger on an Adobe house his father owned and rented out. His father decided it was a good lesson for Marshal and Reuben to buy the cow and chickens and the household would buy the milk and eggs from the boys. However, soon the milk dried up on the cow and a bunch of neighborhood boys stole all the chickens. That was the end of that enterprise, but it taught the boys a valuable lesson. In 1882, Marshal attended the University of the Pacific in Stockton, the first of the family to go to college. After graduation, he joined in the Hale Bros. partnership at the Sacramento store.

We were given a handwritten story by a Juanita Cox after my father died via The Reverend Alanson Higbie, our Episcopal minister, the letter had no date. Juanita's parents lived in a tent on Hunters Point, just south of San Francisco on the bay. There were no houses there then and her father worked in the shipyards. They then moved to a rented house about a mile away and her father wanted to get a better job at the Oyster Point shipyards. He felt he needed a new suit so he could make a good impression. So, her mother started out walking to Mission St. It was very muddy and a carriage pulled up next to her and the gentleman said, "What are you doing walking in the mud? Get in so I can give you a ride." She told him where she was going and why. The man pulled up to a store named Hale's Haberdashery on Mission. He unlocked the door and showed her the suits. She chose a nice brown suit and Mr. Hale wrapped up the suit in a tissue lined box and presented it to her. He said, "This I give you." He would not take her money. "Maybe this will bring me luck." Many years later, she guessed it did. Her father got the job at Oyster's Point and built a house for his family surrounded by a beautiful garden of flowers. We are not sure if this was our grandfather or one of his older brothers, yet we think it was Marshal (II).

*** ***

Marshal (II) took charge of the Hale office in New York for a few years while Prentis Cobb was recovering from Typhoid fever. On January 19, 1898, he married **Mae Baxter Miller Hale – (1872-1948).** They had Marshal Hale, Jr, not the third, since his grandfather was deceased, on October 27, 1902. Seven years later they had Randolph Miller Hale on July 26, 1909.

***

Ophelia Goddard Miller (dates unknown)

Mae Baxter Miller Hale – (1872-1948)

Mae's parents were Ophelia Goddard Miller and Randolph Cotter Miller.

Marshal Hale (II) served as a major for the Red Cross in charge of the Pacific Division, which included California and was stationed in Paris during World War II for eight months. This was at the same time my other grandfather, Jay Clay Powers served in Paris as a major in the Army. My mother often wondered if they had met each other at a restaurant or an officer's club.

Randolph Cotter Miller (dates unknown)

Marshal (II) wrote "Experiences and Reminiscences" of his time (June to December 1918) in England and France for the American Red Cross. He was there before America entered the war, but Americans had been signing up in the French and English armies to fight.

This is an excerpt from his paper. This excerpt describes his visit to a cemetery for the funeral of an American soldier fighting in the French army.

"I noticed a great many French women and a few old men at the cemetery at Suresnes, and as we were about to go, I asked the sergeant what they were doing there. He said they were French men and women of the neighborhood who took charge of two or three or more of the graves. I noticed that the graves were covered with fresh flowers: shrubs and plants were planted around the graves, and on each little cross was the metal disc with the number of the soldier who had died, so that his grave could be located. Underneath the metal disc on each grave was a paper, and on it was written the name of the French man or woman who deemed it a privilege to care for that particular grave. The sergeant said: 'See that old man with the gray mustache, standing over there? He has taken charge of 12 graves.' They were well kept, and seemed to be cared for better than the rest. The sergeant said: 'See the two end graves! He has placed on each an iron vase, about 14 inches high. These vases, he took from his own wife's grave and brought them here for the use of the American soldiers.' Several of the French women were working, fixing up the graves. "Our boys were wounded and died, that Paris might be saved, and these French peasants seemed to appreciate the sacrifice that had been made, and were there caring for the graves in the drizzling rain," Marshal wrote.

In these memoirs, he also writes about the hospitals and multiple wards. We would now call these patients amputees. Their artificial limbs were made of wood, but moveable with joints. The men who stayed in the hospital for six months or more learned to adapt very nicely to their new limbs. They could run and jump, play golf, etc. He remarked that it was a shame our men were released from the service immediately after recovering from the initial injury. It would have been better to keep them in the service, and in the facility so they would learn how to use their new limb. That is a great idea, because we all know, many men came back and discarded their limb because it "bothered" them, or made them fall. They hadn't stayed long enough to learn how to use it, to be comfortable with it. They were also trained in jobs, and upon release, many made a greater income than they had before they lost their limb. As the war went on, I assume this became impossible to maintain with so many amputees. But, even today, we could take a lesson from this, I think.

Marshall II served on the 1915 World Exhibition Committee of San Francisco. The Panama Pacific International Exhibition was our great Uncle Reuben's idea. He lobbied all the way to Washington DC to have it held in San Francisco, and he chaired the committee. Marshal (II) also was on the Board of Bank of America among many others, and was a Bohemian. His best friend was A. P. Giannini, founder of Bank of America and Marshal, Jr. (III) would be a pall bearer at his funeral. When Marshal II was the head of the Republican State Central Committee for the state of California and asked to run for Governor, Mae said if he won, she would take the boys to London for the duration and put them in Eaton for school. Marshal stated that if the phone rang one more time, he was going to accept. It didn't ring, we suspect that perhaps my grandmother had taken the phone off the hook?

On another note, the famous San Francisco Opera Co. was founded at Mae's dining room table on the Presidio Terrace. And, when my grandparents died, the opera house wanted their baby grand piano, a 1918 Steinway, since it had near perfect pitch. My mother didn't want to give it up. To this day, when I have the piano tuned the person will ask if they can stay and play it.

Marshal (II) was also president of Liberty Bank, which was owned by the Bank of Italy, then becoming the Bank of America. He was at one time president of the Downtown Merchants Assn., president of the State Board Harbor Commissioners, president of San Francisco Retail Dry Goods Assn, president of the California Retail Assn., and vice-president of the National Retail Dry Goods Assn. He was known as a man full of vigor, wit, and wisdom.

Another notable contribution was his association with Hahnemann Homeopathic Hospital on California Street. I am not sure if he was an original founder in 1887, or he was just an enormous influencer. He served on the board for many years, as did Marshal (III). In 1978, the hospital was renamed in honor of my grandfather and my father to Marshal Hale Memorial Hospital. It was quite the ceremony. I, also served on the board of the hospital for about ten years. Marshal Hale Memorial Hospital was later taken over by California Pacific Medical Center which was across the street.

CHAPTER 5
MARSHAL III

Marshal Hale, Jr. (III) (1902-1989)

M
arshal Hale, Jr. (III) (1902-1989) since his grandfather was deceased, he was named Marshal, Jr. and not the III, but here the (III) will help differentiate all the Marshals.

Marshal was born in the Fuller house (Fuller Paints) as his parent's home was

Marshal and Mae

being built in the Presidio Terrace in San Francisco on October 27, 1902. He was affectionately known as Marchie by those close when he was a child. In April of 1906 his parents decided to travel to Europe and left Marshal with a nanny in San Francisco. They got as far as Denver, when on April 19, 1906, the earthquake struck San Francisco. They returned immediately, and ventured on the trip again the following year, taking my father with them.

My father and his brother had a nanny named Rosina Franz from Holland. She lived with the family and when the boys were grown they got her an apartment in San Francisco and supported her for the rest of her life. I remember visiting her there, and she would spend every Christmas with us. She passed away about 1957. Her urn is in the family crypt at Cypress Lawn. She was truly family.

Marshal (III) attended Potter School, in San Francisco, where he learned to love poetry and creative writing. He wrote many stories, some of which are still at our ranch. He then attended Stanford University graduating in 1924 majoring in pre-law. He was asked to join Sigma Nu fraternity and during the hazing he had to wear three little bells tied with a string around his penis for 3 days. The very young and attractive female Spanish teacher wanted to know what all the jingling was about when he

Marshal, Randolph, Marshal

moved in his classroom seat and demanded he hand over the bells. Of course, she thought they were in his pocket. He said he couldn't do that and she asked to speak to him after class. Fortunately, one of his fraternity mates was in the same class and explained the situation to the very embarrassed young teacher.

They also had to steal a turkey from a turkey ranch, there were several surrounding Stanford in those days. Dad along with a rather small classmate managed to get into the pen. They grabbed the turkey, then my father boosted the smaller gent holding the twenty-five plus pound turkey up over the fence. The turkey took off in flight with the young man dangling below and flew about 20 feet before landing! Next, they had to get it back to the fraternity house. So, they tied a rope

around its neck and drove back in a convertible with the turkey flying above them. After that, Marshal's name to his fraternity brothers, was Squawk! My mother never quite believed this story until she met Dick Highland and he confirmed this and another great story that will come up next. While at Stanford, Marshal played Freshman football and then excelled in track and field. He was captain of the track

team in 1924 and went to the Olympics in Paris as one of the favorites to win. He roomed with Dick Highland in a second story flat. They trained all day, and then at night would take a taxi to the famous Montmartre district in Paris. That was where the best nightclubs were in 1924. At night, the cabbies would put a black hood over the meter and would barter for a higher price. Parisians would pay double the daytime fee, but the foreigners were held up for whatever the cabbie could extract. After the first week, my father and Dick got wise. They would agree to whatever the cabbie requested and then pay exactly double the daytime fee, run into the hotel locking the front door behind them. The taxi driver would yell and scream and bang on the front door waking everyone up. The boys devised a plan. Before they left for the night they would each fill their basin (large bowl) with a pitcher of water, since there was no running water in their rooms. They carried the basins out to the balcony and sat them on the corner of the rod iron balcony railing. Upon their return, they would run upstairs, out to the balconies, and dump the water on the cab driver. He would muter a few obscenities and then quietly go away. This worked night after night until the bowl slipped out of Dick's hands and knocked the cab driver out cold below.

During the training my father pulled his ham string. Although the favorite for the 100-yard dash along with the University of California (Berkeley) track star, Charlie Paddock, my father did not recover in time to race in the Olympics. He had beaten

Charlie that year in the Stanford/Cal races, and therefore could possibly have gotten the Gold Medal. As you recall from the movie, "Chariots of Fire", Harold Abrahams, from the University of Cambridge, false started twice. The third time you are disqualified. Dad was sitting in box seats next to Douglas Fairbanks, Jr. and swore Abrahams false started the third time as well. He always wanted to meet Fairbanks again and ask him what he thought. I've watched the videos now on YouTube, I don't think he false started the third time, but perhaps my father still would have beaten him and gotten the Gold, or at least the Silver?

Shortly after graduating from Stanford, Marshal became a founding member of the San Jose Junior Chamber of Commerce and served as its board president. He then managed the San Jose Hale's store. In November of 1930, he went to run a store in Hollywood, Robertson's, that was separate from Hale Bros. Marshal (II) and Marshal (III) purchased the controlling shares in this store and my father became president. This is where he met my mother, more on that later. They bought the store during the depression and didn't anticipate the depression lasting so long. They had to gross $2,000 per day and they were only averaging $1500. To give you a perspective, neck ties and girls dresses were $1, women's dresses were on average $5.75. One interesting story that came from letters between my father and grandfather was that on February 29, 1932, a leap year, the store was entirely run by women. My father commented to his father about the great job they did!

By 1934 they had to sell it and the inventory, overall losing only about $30k. After Hollywood, he became an executive with Montgomery Wards in New York and later went into the Mail Order office in Chicago. There was a bar that he frequented where often the same men would go night after night. He became friendly with several of the men until he suddenly put two and two together and realized he had been hanging out with Al Capone's men!

He returned to Hale Bros in San Francisco in 1938, the same year he married Lucille Powers. They honeymooned in Carmel, CA and then returned to San

Francisco. He was soon called to serve as Deputy Chief of the Textile Division of the Office of Production Management in Washington, DC. He was called a "Dollar a Year Man" because that is exactly what he was paid, and they even took the tax out of the $1 check! While serving for the war effort he had to call the First Lady, Eleanor Roosevelt, and ask her to please stop having all the wives and mothers knit socks for their "boys" at war. They were not regulation, would not fit in the boots, and they were depleting the wool supply desperately needed for uniforms and blankets. Mrs. Roosevelt said, "Why, by all means, Mr. Hale, and I am so sorry! I'll send out the word right away."

My father told another story. I'm not sure if I have this exactly right, but the men in the ship yards of New York were always cleaning the hulls of the ships to remove the barnacles. One day, a man realized they were adhered so tight to the ships that it was very difficult to pry them off. He thought this could be used as an adhesive to adhere objects together. And, soon a better "glue" was to be had for the war effort.

The three cousins Prentis, Newton, and Marshal (II)) ran Hale Bros., but also had a real estate holding company known as Hale Assoc. It owned land in many different areas in northern California including the Sacramento area. Hale Associates owned the land that the El Dorado Hills development was built on just east of Sacramento in the 1960's. I remember touring the development when there were only ten houses built of the master plan.

There was a falling out among Prentice, Newton and my father. Newton sided with Prentis and in 1957, my father basically retired. He maintained an office in the headquarters but did not work in the day to day operations. He remained on the Hale Bros. and Hale Assoc. boards and was an active board member to Hahnemann Hospital, Transamerica, the Salvation Army, and to Bank of America.

Hale Bros. purchased The Broadway in southern California and Emporium Capwell's in northern California in the early 1960's. Then they purchased Neiman

Marcus, Sunset House and Waldon Books in the early 1970's. The company changed their name to Carter Hawley Hale to reward two long time executives. I went to that shareholders meeting, I thought the name change sounded like a law firm. The company then expanded to include Bergdorf Goodman's in New York, Holt-Reinfew in Canada, and Thalmeier's in London. My father thought they were expanding too quickly. Perhaps, if he had still been in charge he would have done things differently, with a better outcome. In 1982, The Limited tried to do a hostile takeover. Although, it didn't happen, the hand writing was on the wall. My sister, Valerie, moving back to California from Colorado, was worried about the stock price dropping if the Limited take-over succeeded. She decided it would be best to sell her stock and was nervous about telling my Dad. He agreed she should. At the same time my husband, Jack, a Financial Advisor and stock broker, said to my father, "Marshal, there's no place in business for sentiment." My father agreed and he sold his stock slowly, as did Loralyn and I. When our father died, many thought we inherited millions. That was not true. We did fine, but most people, just because of the family history, greatly exaggerated the truth. This was not something perpetuated by any of us, it was just assumed.

Prentis Cobb Hale was not the kind, benevolent, generous man of his ancestor's ilk. He was an unfaithful husband, absentee father by his own children's admission, and a selfish, disgruntled greedy man. In his later years after Newton and my father passed away, if I was in Neiman Marcus (where his office was then located) he would seek me out. It was strange and interesting. He would invite me to his office or come find me in the rotunda restaurant. I had always loved the tiger rug in his office as a child. I hadn't seen it in years until the first time he invited me up in the 1980's. I was curious about him so I always accepted his invitation. I had heard all the stories about him. And, let me tell you these are not tame stories. His wife, Pat, and mother of his children committed suicide when I was seventeen in his dressing room with his gun. He was having an affair with Denise Minelli, and I remember, just a few months after Pat's suicide, being in a cab with my parents in London and my father opening the London Times and reading that he had married Denise. My father was disgusted and upset. My cousin, Linda Hale Buckley, wrote a scathing book about her father. And yet, he was always so kind to me? He would ask me how I was and about my sisters. It was very odd, the only thing I could figure was that he had regrets that he was estranged from his daughters and sons in his waning years, and wished he had maybe done things differently. I don't know if this is a correct assumption.

There will be more later about my father and mother and his later life. My father passed away with his dog licking his face on his bed at the age of 86 in 1989.

Eulogy for Marshal Hale III
Written by Charise Hale McHugh
Delivered by Dr. John M. Weinmann

No one could ever say our father didn't live a full and interesting life. He was born in San Francisco in 1902 and was raised on the Presidio Terrace. He remembers sneaking down to his basement at night and hearing Chinese servants having their Tong meetings and smoking Opium. His parents left for Europe shortly before the Earthquake hit in 1906, they returned immediately, and took him with them the following year. That was his first introduction to one of his great loves, traveling and Europe. Our Father carried around the history of England on a card in his wallet from Egbert to Queen Elizabeth. He said he could put whatever was happening in any given year anywhere in the world in perspective by correlating it with English history. Daddy went on to Potter School and then Stanford. He shocked his father by playing freshman football and made him very proud by going on to becoming Captain of the Stanford Track Team and heading for Paris for the 1924 Olympics. The antics of his friends and he, let loose on Paris night life for a summer, are very entertaining and often comical. He pulled his hamstring in preliminaries (in which he had the best time, by the way) kept him from competing in the actual games. He had to be content with watching from the sidelines next to a very young Douglas Fairbanks Jr. When Daddy was 22 he became a member of the Bohemian Club. He stayed a member for 65 years. He was a member of Dragon's Camp and worked in many, many shows. One of his proudest achievements was a dramatic exhausting dance all over the stage. The then Prince of Sweden (later the King) said it was the most magnificent thing he had ever seen. He went on to play many roles, dancing and singing and including yes, once a woman. He shared with us many memories of pranks and such, that he would tell with a twinkle in his eye and a devilish smile. He would not work for Hale Brothers until he learned the ropes "elsewhere". So, he went to Chicago and worked for Montgomery Wards. He made his mark in new innovative marketing through the catalog lay ups and special merchandizing techniques. While with Monkey Wards he frequented a pub that was also a favorite of some of Capone's men. He also spent a memorable summer back packing on horseback through Yellowstone National Park for six weeks. When he got to Old Faithful he dropped his laundry in and twenty minutes later it shot up in a spray of water and he caught the whitest brightest boxer shorts you ever saw! After returning from Chicago he began working for his father. He made friends with the people on the roof of the store that operated RKO, one of San Francisco's first radio stations. Many pleasant hours were spent listening to beautiful voices of their talented singers, thus launching another lifelong passion for good music and opera. He traveled to Los Angeles to take over a store down there and met a beautiful young blonde actress complaining to the manager that she had an opening to go to and for the first time could not find anything appropriate to wear! "I wish those Hales had stayed in San Francisco", she said. When she was all through the manager said, "Miss Powers allow me to introduce you to Mr. Hale". They were married in 1938. They found the most beautiful property they could find and broke ground on Tiptoe Lane in November 1941, thus launching another lifelong love affair with the flora and fauna of Northern California. After completing a home of all windows and only one complete standing wall built around his beloved oak trees as not to harm them, he launched another career as a private landscape architect of his own rolling six acres. "Enchantara" the enchanted forest". The war began and Daddy was off to work as a dollar a year man in Washington D.C. for the war effort. We were very short on wool, and all the wives and mothers were replenishing our supply further by knitting items that could not be worn by the boys overseas. A phone call was made to the head of the Red Cross and after explaining the serious problem, Eleanor Roosevelt promised our father that she would correct the matter immediately. Daddy returned to Hillsborough to a partially completed Tiptoe Lane with his dollar a year check in hand – well it was more like eighty-two cents, because Uncle Sam felt a need to tax that dollar. Loralyn was born in May of 1941, and Valerie, a Valentine baby in 1943, then Marsha, a fellow Scorpio, in 1944. They were so cute, all dressed alike and would all sit together on Daddy's lap while he read them a story. They were the apple of his eye. In 1948, Daddy and Mother bought the ranch. What a blessing for four girls born in Hillsborough. We had our horses, we worked, we *could identify and use such indispensable tools as a linoleum knife and a sickle. It was the best thing he could ever have done for us. We learned to work hard (with mild complaining) and he instilled strong work ethics and character. We built rooms, tore out barns, reroofed buildings and one of us delighted in always volunteering to go get the lemonade! Hopefully, we're passing the same traditions on to our children, on that same Sierra land. Four years after purchasing the ranch the milk man was shocked to receive an order of skim milk. Yes, Mother nodded, AGAIN. Charise was born in September of 1952 right before Marshal's 50th birthday! The travels begin…Disneyland, Hawaii, Europe, the Orient, the Middle and Near East, Mexico, China, Central America, and the land Down Under. This became more than a passion, it became a lifelong love with foreign lands, their people, food, culture, and history. They delighted in taking their grandchildren, and Daddy, after Mother died, traveled with us and our husbands. He loved each of his grandchildren individually – John Michael, David, Kevin, Paul, Allen, Valerie, Byron, Marlena, Tamara, Melanie and Joshua. He leaves with us, and them, a strong honest character to deal with all people fairly and equally, to remain level headed and above all never lose our sense of humor! We lost our Father, and the world lost a very special man, but knowing he is reunited with our Mother is very consoling. Look out world, together they may work a lot of miracles.*

CHAPTER 6
RANDOLPH

Randolph Miller Hale 1909-1974. Our father's brother was born seven years after Marshal. He was run over by a streetcar as a child and they grafted skin from our father's leg to his. Impressive for around 1915. Randolph attended Harvard University majoring in drama and set off for Broadway to pursue an acting career. He acted on Broadway in "Happy Landing" (1932) and "We, The People" (1933). He also later produced two Broadway productions; "On Borrowed Time" (1953) and "Bicycle Race to Nevada" (1963). Around 1934 he decided to devote his time fully to merchandising. He became an executive of McCrearey's Store in New York City where he gained experience. In 1935, he returned to San Francisco to go into the family's department store business, ultimately becoming the head of women's fashion. Although, he seemed to have a real knack for it, it just wasn't his cup of tea, and left merchandising once more to pursue a theatrical career.

Marjorie Lord Hale (1918-2015) and Randolph Miller Hale (1909-1974)

He was married to Jean Gilbert on July 6, 1940 and had two children, **Randi Jean Hale, October 19,1941** and **Dyckman Gilbert Hale, on May 3, 1944**. Randi married **Howard Alan Huenergardt** and they had **Charles Marshal Huenergardt (12/12/1976-)**. Charlie married **Mary Jane Ashford (1979-)**. They have twins **Loula Jean and Haley Jane Huenergardt (6/8/2009-)** and **Daisy Anne Huenergardt (9/1/2010-)**. Dyckman married Colleen Walsh and they also had twins, **Sarah Christine Hale and Daniel Gilbert Hale (10/10/1984-)**.

Jean and Randolph divorced in 1954 or 1955. In July of 1952, Randolph leased the Alcazar Theatre in San Francisco. Among the actors who performed there were David Niven, Dianna Lynn, and Scott Brady. In a production called "Three for Tonight" were dancers Marge and Gower Champion and Harry Belafonte. It was here that he met Marjorie Lord (1918-2015). She was the television star of the 1950's series "Make Room for Daddy" starring Danny Thomas. He married Marjorie in 1958. At the Alcazar, she starred in the comedy favorite, "Anniversary Waltz", that ran for two years. The theater was a part of the New York Theatre Guild and big name stars became regulars on the Alcazar marquee. The final production was "Rhinoceros", staring Zero Mostel in 1961. The theater was subsequently torn down by the property owners.

Randolph then opened a theater-in-the-round in 1964 in Woodland Hills, in the San Fernando Valley. His partners were Bob Hope and Art Linkletter and it was called The Valley Music Theatre. My mother and I traveled to Los Angeles to tour the studios in 1964 and were lucky enough to see John Raitt in "Oklahoma" complete with him entering the theater on horseback, singing the title song, down the main isle. When we were in Randolph's office we met his dog, Rocky, a Dalmatian. I said something funny and my uncle said, "That's funny, Rocky, don't you think? Laugh, Rocky." And, with that the dog proceeded to raise his upper lips, hiss through his teeth, bob his head and shoulders as though he was laughing like a human. That's really the only memory I have of my uncle.

PART II

MARSHAL AND LUCILLE

CHAPTER 7
MARSHAL AND LUCILLE

About 1932, my mother had a movie premiere to go to and needed a dress. She went into her favorite department store, Robertson's in Hollywood, and could not find anything appropriate. After searching the entire department, she went downstairs and ran into the store manager standing with a young gentleman. She said, "Mr. (Smith), I have always been able to come into this store at the last minute and find the prefect dress I need. Today, I could find nothing, I'm so frustrated, I wish those Hales would have stayed in San Francisco!" With that, the store manager said, "Miss Powers, I would like to introduce you to Marshal Hale." Of course, she blushed and felt terribly embarrassed. At which time, my father said, "Miss Powers, I am going on a buying trip to New York next week, and if you would kindly tell me what you are looking for, I would happily buy whatever you wish." Suave guy, my dad. My father, as promised brought some gowns to my mother's house and he met my mother's mother. But, they didn't start dating until much later.

Earlier, Marshal Hale (III) had fallen in love with a concert pianist who chose her career over life with my father. Being his first real love, he was deeply hurt by the breakup. He married Helen Savage in 1931 while at Robertson's. He was on the rebound, as they say, and I guess she didn't think the fact that she had tuberculosis, and could not ever have children, was something she should tell her future husband. Things went bad right out of the gate, and when my father discovered she had

Wedding photos, 1938

hidden this fact from him, that was pretty much it. However, they were married for 7 years, but only lived together for 7 weeks. Grandmother Hale was not pleased that Marshal might get a divorce. Quite scandalous at that time and in those social circles. He was still married to Helen when he met my mother.

Years later, my mother would meet "the other Mrs. Hale" at a San Francisco luncheon. They became great friends. Helen and Lucille spoke on the telephone and exchanged letters my entire childhood. Helen remarried, finally, in 1971, my father had paid alimony to her every month for over forty years.

My grandmother was also not pleased when my father started dating an actress. In those days, a Hollywood actress was considered a slight step higher than a prostitute. Just to give you an idea of the stuffiness of my grandparents, when my mother was pregnant with my oldest sister, Loralyn, she announced it in the living room to both my grandfather and my grandmother. Mae was shocked, and my mother soon found out that she should have told my grandmother in private, and then Mae would have told my grandfather in private.

Twink

While dating, my parents had spider monkeys. "Twink" would rest in between the buttons of my father's double breasted suit coat. One time they were sitting at a bar and a rather obnoxious patron said something like, "Oh, I suppose you could pull a rabbit out of your hat.'" My father replied, "No, but would this due?". He reached in his coat and pulled Twink out and set him on the bar. Twink ran up and down the bar stealing all the olives and cherries out of the drinks and preceded to get quite intoxicated himself.

***

Lucille and Marshal married in Stanford Chapel and had their reception in the home of a friend in Burlingame on November 12, 1938. The wedding was attended

by his parents and brother, Randolph, and his wife Jean and a few friends. My mother wore a purple dress, purple was quite the rage that year. Forty-six years later, I would marry in that same dress to Jack.

They lived on Hillside Circle, Burlingame while building a home in Hillsborough on six acres of an oak tree forest. Dad purchased the land from Hale Associates, their real estate holding company, had the street built and named it Tiptoe Lane. The house was named "Enchantara", enchanted house. My father had a very whimsical sense of humor. The house was very modern for its time, all glass and only one complete wall that was in the living room where the fire place was located. Designed by Clarence W. W. Mayhew (1906-1994), it was featured in Architectural Digest (May 1949) as the cover story. The glass was floor to ceiling and in the living room two panes of glass came together with just

Lucille and Marshal laying on the spot that would become their bedroom at Tiptoe Lane

three small metal brackets holding them in place. The house was about 4500 square feet and was built around the oak trees, only one was cut down to build it. It was started the November before Pearl Harbor and completed in June of 1942. They moved in before it was quite completed and my mother would have to be up and dressed by 6AM when the workers arrived because without drapes and so many windows, there was no place she could have privacy. They had separate dressing rooms, and my father had a window in his shower. When they were walking through the framed house and looking at the blue prints, my mother exclaimed, "But, Clarence, he can't have a window in his shower just 40 feet from the front door?"

Tiptoe Lane, Enchantara

Clarence replied, "Goodness gracious Lucille, Marshal isn't THAT tall!" And, so when I would walk to the bus stop every morning I would wave to my father taking a shower, the third of the smaller windows from the left.

The house and property were amazing. My father should have been a landscape architect. He was very good at it. We had camellia and rhododendron bushes that were 15 feet tall and you could climb them. There was a large lawn, dwarf maples, seasonal flowers, perennials, ivy, jade trees, gorgeous azaleas, lilies of the valley,

View of side of the house with pool

daphnia, and lush ferns that dotted the Live Oak forest. There were paths everywhere and steps made of railway ties. There were also patios, gravel landings, and sandstone walls.

✳ ✳ ✳

Kay Haraguchi was our gardener every Tuesday and Thursday for 40 years. He had been raised in Hawaii and when his father came from Japan to visit he would bring him with him to the house. I laughed one day when I heard him trying to speak to his own father. Kay didn't speak Japanese very well and his father spoke no English. I considered Kay a second father. in a way, and also a best friend. I used to love to be sick on a Tuesday or Thursday so I could go out and help him. We had this game that, I think, started with my sisters. I would steal his hat and throw it up in a tree, and he would have to go get a long bamboo pole to get it down. He never complained at the annoyance, he would just laugh. I adored him. My father helped him buy his first

Katsu (Kay) Haraguchi, 1984

house in Foster City, which was built in the early 1960's. It was one of the first planned communities and built entirely on fill in the bay. He and his wife, Tatsu, lived there until they died in the late 1990's.

In 1968 we added a pool, and once again my father couldn't do an ordinary pool. No, he designed it himself, a freelance pond shape with rock around the edges and a low step in the deep end so you could rest or observe a diver. It was a wonderful rock edged curved design. He did two sets of marble stairs down to the pool area and built the pool house himself. It housed the pool equipment and had a small dressing room as well. He was a fair carpenter as well as landscaper. I remember helping him build, both at the Ranch and at Tiptoe Lane, and landscape the gardens around the pool with retaining walls and borders.

My father passed away on January 29, 1989 laying back on his bed with the dog licking his face. At the age of 86, he hadn't been to a doctor in over five years, so they had to do an autopsy. He was riddled with cancer. The only complaint he made, was while staying with us over Christmas, he complained of a back ache. But, what a way to go, no doctor appointments for over five years! Not many of us can say that!

Life Skills learned from my father

Live by these words: honesty, trust, and integrity. Don't lend money to friends or relatives. Your doctor and lawyer should be younger than you are. The male always walks on the street side. When in a race, stay behind the first or second place runner until the last half a lap, then pour on the steam. And, when swimming the Freestyle stroke, you don't have to take your mouth all the way out of the water, half way will due, you won't breath in the water, air is lighter. Always leave a good tip. When

Lucille and Marshal, 1965

dancing, stay on the balls of your feet and feel your partner's rhythm. Pay all your bills on time and don't incur much debt.

Life Skills learned from my mother

Always kiss someone good-bye and say, "I love you." You never know when you won't get another chance. Never cut a potato, muffin or biscuit with a knife, it packs it so it's no longer fluffy. Use a fork. When someone is angry at you don't be angry back, they think they are justified in being angry. Talk to them as though butter would melt in your mouth and acknowledge you understand why they are angry. Hang sheer draperies wet after washing. If you have a critter in the house, throw a wet washcloth over them, then scoop them up and throw it and the washcloth outside. Never procrastinate, it will just make it harder. You don't have to iron placemats and napkins, just smooth them out wet on a smooth surface and let them dry. They will appear as though they have been starched and pressed. Cut flowers at an angle before arranging and pour some 7-Up into the water. Keep a dry towel in the dryer, your cloths will dry faster. She was Miss Emily Post when it came to Etiquette, and taught me to write a thank you note right away. And, she taught numerous make-up tricks from her Hollywood years.

***

I would be remiss if I didn't tell you a little about Nana (Martha) and Occi (Oscar). She was the only "grandmother" and he "grandfather" I had. My grandparents either died before any of us were born, or when my sisters were very young. Nana was hired as a nanny when Loralyn was a baby and Tiptoe Lane was about to be finished. Nana had been a nurse in Germany. My parents also hired Occi to do odd jobs around the house. Being a new house, there were plenty. In Germany, Occi had owned a clothes pattern factory and made a very nice living. My father helped Occi get a job, first at Hale Bros, then at Montgomery Wards. He eventually became the manager of the paint department there. They moved to an apartment in Burlingame, and later bought a nice duplex house. I have no memory of life without Nana and Occi. They had no children of their own.

Nana was born in Leipzig, Germany, (east Germany from 1963-1991). Every time she went to visit her sister, we held our breath until her return. Occi was born of Jewish decent in Vienna, Austria. He was persecuted before WWII and their house was marked that a Jew lived there. Nana had to wear a sign around her neck that she was married to a Jew. She was sat up in a store front window for the people to throw tomatoes at her. The Germans entered Occi's home and emptied all his books from his library onto the floor and lit a match. That was when they knew they had to get out of Germany. Nana had gone to school with Rudolph Hess (deputy fuhrer to Adolf Hitler (1933-1941) and he had a crush on her. He helped them get out. She put her jewelry in her vagina so it wouldn't be found when they were searched. They had packed up fifteen trunks of belongings but only three or four made it to New York.

Oscar (1898-1974) and Martha Blum (1902-1989) Wonderful Friends, no relation

They came to work for the family right before Tiptoe Lane was completed in 1942. Later, Nana came every Thursday and every other Sun when the maid was off to fix dinner. Occi came on the Sundays as he was off work.

Later, after I was born, they would come to dinner every Thursday night and I would run out to greet them knowing Nana would have a treat for me. Usually, a cube of sugar. They spent every Christmas Eve with us and visited at the Ranch every summer. We all loved them dearly, it would have been impossible to love grandparents any more.

CHAPTER 8
THE HALE GIRLS

LORALYN HALE WAGNER (1941-)

Loralyn was born May 27, 1941. (None of us had middle names). She attended South, and later North, Hillsborough Schools and then Castilleja High School and met her future husband, **John Wagner (9/7/1939-1/17/1998)**, a Marine, and married at the age of 19. She attended Cal Berkley, and then San Francisco State, and majored in Sociology. They lived for a short time in San Francisco and then settled in Santa Rosa and later built a spectacular house amid a redwood forest in

John Wagner (1939-1998) and Loralyn Hale Wagner (1941-)

Paul, David, Kevin, Loralyn, Johnny, John

Sebastapol. Loralyn and Johnny have four sons, **John Michael Wagner (3/21/1964-), David Hale Wagner (3/27/1967-), Kevin Mark Wagner (10/9/1968-), and Paul Clay Wagner (7/28/1971-)**.

John Michael's children are **Robin Aileen Wagner (1/8/1996-) and Michael John Wagner (7/11/1997-)**.

Loralyn, John Michael, Dylan, Friend, Michael, Friend, Robin

David's children are twins **Cooper Hale Wagner (11/30/2010-) and Caitlyn Carmi Wagner (11/30/2010-)**.

Kevin's children are **Emily Anne Wagner (3/31/1997-), Dylan Mark Wagner (9/6/2002-),** and **Nigel Alexander Wagner (9/6/2002-)**.

Paul and Trina did not have children, but were wonderful Foster parents to two girls, and helped raise numerous kids in the neighborhood who are still all close to them today.

Johnny died at the age of fifty-five from hydro syphilitics. Johnny was one of the funniest people I ever met. He just had this quick whit and sharp sense of humor.

Emily, David, Cooper, Povi, Caitlyn, Loralyn, Capri Wippich, Dylan, Kevin, Nigel (back), Spencer Wippich, Susan, Trina, Paul, 2012

My sister now lives in an Asian inspired A-frame not far from their forest house in Occidental.

This is not meant to be a biography of my sisters. I will leave that to them. However, I would like to mention my favorite memories since these are my stories.

Favorite Wagner memories

My sister reading me the Bible on her bed every night when I was five, dropping a lizard down her back at the Ranch (mean little kid), Loralyn teaching me to cook (I can make the best gravy without lumps), it was watching my brother-in-law tackle my sister and tickle her until we were all crying with laughter, them addressing Christmas presents to each other with the names To: Nose, From: Feet, going on tow truck runs with Johnny when he did that as a second job, Johnny teaching me Judo in their back yard when I was twelve, and John Michael watching from the living room window yelling to his mother, "Mommy, Mommy, Auntie Fweece fipped Daddy!" Loralyn teaching me, or was it brainwashing me to have natural childbirth (it worked, I did), and having a whole set of babies to play with and dote on starting when I was age eleven. I didn't need dolls, I had real babies!

As for the natural childbirth, as I say, she started having her boys when I was eleven, by the time I was having Byron at twenty-three, I was indoctrinated. It wasn't until the morning I was in labor and asking about the timing of contractions, that she said, as we were hanging up, "Oh, yeah, by the way, it hurts like hell, like being stabbed with a hot knife!" Thank you, Loralyn, I did find that out, but wouldn't have had it any other way. I loved being able to get up and walk down the hall after the baby was born to look at him/her without feeling groggy. And, that is what I remember Loralyn doing every time. I also thank Loralyn for getting me through some tough family times at home and having me take the bus up to Santa Rosa many weekends when my parents were drinking. She was a sister and mentor all rolled into one. I absolutely idolized my brother-in-law and still miss him very much. I had no brothers, Johnny came into my life at five. I have very few memories without him.

✳ ✳ ✳

VALERIE HALE GILLUM (1943 -)
Valerie was born February 14, 1943, on her paternal grandfather's (Marshal Hale (II)) birthday and, of course, Valentine's Day. She was precocious and didn't walk

until she was almost two and then got up and ran! She attended South, North, and West Hillsborough Schools, and then Castilleja High School for her first two years of high school, and then Burlingame High so she could be at the same school as her younger sister, Marsha. Valerie attended Stockton College and later San Diego State.

Delbert Ray Gillum (1941-2016) and Valerie Hale Gillum (1943-)

She met her husband at seventeen, **Delbert Ray Gillum (Dobie) (4/16/1941-12/18/2016)** who was serving in the Navy. They married when Valerie was twenty-three, longest engagement in history.

Dobie and Valerie have three girls: **Valyrie Gillum (8/13/1974-)**, **Marlena Gillum (4/9/1976-)**, both adopted, and then at almost forty, Valerie had **Melanie Gillum Hanan (1/26/1983-)**. My mother had died the previous year and we are sure she got up to heaven and said, "I want my daughter pregnant and I want it now!" 6 months later, she was pregnant.

Wedding 11/26/1966

Valyrie's children are **Nathan Hunter Friedman (5/19/2005-)** and **Hannah Charlotta Friedman (9/25/2007-)**.

Marlena's child is **Noelle Garielle Kemery (11/18/2004-)**

Melanie at this writing has no children.

Dobie passed away in 2016, fifty-six years to the day of their meeting, of Pancreatic cancer, and it was the most incredible death. It's hard to explain, but we all knew almost to the day, but he was not in any pain and he was lucid till the last morning. We all got to say our good-byes. I must put in this story, this would only happen to my sister. Marlena had asked her Dad to give them a sign that he got up to heaven all right one day before his passing. Dobie passes away and the hearse is called from the funeral home. They load Dobie in and, of course, Valerie and the girls are crying. Then the driver goes to start up the hearse and it won't start. Dead battery. My sister says. "No problem, I have jumper cables right here!" She turns

Dobie, Valyrie, Nathan, Hannah, Melanie, Noelle, Marlena, Valerie

around her Subaru, attaches the cables because the driver has them backwards, and orders the man to start his engine. It starts up fine and off he goes. At that point, my sister and nieces all burst out laughing. Marlena says, "Nice one dad, okay we got it, you made it up there and mom is going to be fine without you." Again, Dobie was like my brother, he met Valerie when I was just eight years old. I am blessed to have had two brothers in my life that I adored. Thank you, sisters.

Favorite Gillum memories

Valerie and I sharing a bedroom and realizing how funny she can be, riding horses and always forging ahead if we could see any light through the tree barriers, sleeping in beds where our heads were at right angles in San Salvador and taking turns sleeping or watching the tarantula on the ceiling over our heads, doing projects at the Ranch, Dobie taking me on awesome motorcycle rides in the hills of San Diego, all of us dune-buggying and laughing all day, Dobie doing his Donald Duck impersonation, doing sit ups at the Ranch with me sitting on his back (aged 8), and eating a dozen tacos, just the two of us at a Riverside road stand. When I was almost thirteen, my parents and I spent the month of August at Vacation Village in San Diego where Valerie and Dobie lived. They came to dinner one night in the hotel restaurant and when dinner was delivered, Dobie picked up the parsley from his plate and said. "Do you belong to the SPPPPPPPP Club?" I said, "What is that?" To which he replied, "The Society of the Prevention of People Putting Parsley on People's Plates in Public Places." I loved it and have every once in while asked the same question. Also, Valerie always being there for me and being a best friend. We can say anything to each other and we know exactly what we mean. Never any judgement. And, for teaching me valuable marriage lessons and the "rules" and "lines drawn" during arguments with your spouse. Thank you, Val, you are probably partially responsible for my long marriage to Jack!

※※※

DAVID HALE (1944-1944)

My parents had a boy that was premature and only lived a few hours. I remember my father telling me that one of the hardest things he ever did was to hail a cab and drive his dead child, who was in a small box next to him in the taxi, to the crematorium. They named him David, thinking they may still have a son to call

Marshal. His ashes were later mixed in with his grandfather's, Marshal Hale II, and is not identified on the front of the family crypt at Cypress Lawn.

✳ ✳ ✳

MARSHA HALE LITKE GORDO (11/14/1944-7/15/1992)

Marsha Hale Litke Gordo (11/14/1944-7/14/1992)

Marsha was born a month premature on November 14, 1944. She attended some special schools as she was growing up and then Burlingame High School. She was not special needs, but she was slow. When my son was eight, he asked me what was wrong with Marsha because he realized that he understood numbers and money better than she did. But, when she put her mind to it, she could accomplish whatever she wanted. She eloped at nineteen with **Fredrick Eugene Daniel Litke, "Jack" (7/10/1943-7/3/1983)**, the boy who lived across the street from us at the Ranch.

They had one son, **Allen Eugene Litke (7/31/1967-12/20/1988)**. They were divorced when Allen was in high school, and she married Glen Gordo, a real piece of work. I thought my Jack was going to crawl under the couch at the Ranch when I told Glen point blank that if anything happened to my sister, her trust was left to her sisters and not to him. There was a lot of speculation about Glen, none of it good, and probably all of it true. Allen died at age twenty-one of an epileptic type seizure in his sleep, in 1988. Marsha was killed along with Glen in an automobile accident in 1992. They had blood alcohol levels of 2.8 and 3.8 respectively. Glen was driving and at that level of alcohol that rendered him almost comatose according to the paramedic. Marsha could not do a lot of things well, but drive a car and shoot a gun, she did very well. Unfortunately, Glen was behind the wheel even though witnesses saw them pulled off the road and arguing, probably about letting her drive. He swerved, or she pulled the wheel, to avoid hitting Marsha's former niece (Jack Litke's niece) head on. The three-day old Ford Ranger truck flipped end over end, over bumper to bumper seven times before coming to rest against a tree on Highway 49 across from the USONA fire station. Marsha was thrown from the car and died in the ambulance on the way to the hospital.

Favorite Marsha memories

Marsha trying to convince me there really was a Santa Claus when at the age of five I had figured it out, playing Cowboys and Indians on horseback at the Ranch (I was always the Indian because I was young enough that I could take off my shirt), watching her shoot a gun, watching all the Navy men line up on the aircraft carrier in Hong Kong with binoculars from our hotel room, our final horseback ride together two months before she died. I have no fond memories of either brother-in-law even though I knew Jack from birth. When I was eleven and she was nineteen we traveled to Palm Springs together, my parents were drinking and couldn't make the New Year's week trip. I handled all the money, the plane tickets, and the checking into the hotel. That was a fun trip together though, until Jack Litke came down and took us to a party for New Year's Eve, and then stuck his tongue down my throat at midnight! I was eleven!!! He thought it was funny. Well, there you go. Marsha was always a challenge and so were her choices. If my parents told her not to do something, you could bet your bottom dollar she would do it. But, she was my sister, and I loved her. And, when she died it was very difficult to get over. I had lost my parents and her son, a nephew, but losing a sibling was very different!

✸✸✸

CHARISE HALE WERNER MCHUGH (9/23/1952-)

I was born on September 23, 1952 when Lucille was almost 41 and Marshal almost 50. I was a very friendly child and loved everyone. I excelled in swimming and learned to ride horses before I could walk. I went to North Hillsborough Elementary School, William H. Crocker Middle School, both in Hillsborough,

Charise Hale Werner McHugh (9/23/1952-) and John Dillon McHugh II (1945-)

California. I went to Castilleja High School for Girls in Palo Alto, California. And was very active in sports and drama. I was also co-chair of the Spirit Club. Then, I attended the University of the Pacific, University of California at Davis, and graduated Cum Laude from College of Notre Dame in 1974 with an MA in History.

I married **Henri Louis "Bud" Werner" (4/14,1950-)** in 1973, and had two children. **Byron Hale Werner (11/30/1975-)** and **Tamara Werner (5/8/1978-)**.

Byron has two children by **Amy Muckinhaupt Werner (11/15/1975-)**, **Annabelle Grace Werner (1/232010-)** and **Sadie Rose Werner (5/30/2012-)**.

Tamara has two children by **Adam Christopher Duarte (10/21/1982-)**, **Jacob Hale Duarte (9/30/2005-)** and **Chloe Jane Duarte (2/14/2007-)**. Tamara and Adam were divorced in 2018.

Bud and I were divorced in 1982 and I met Jack McHugh later that year. We

Charise, Valerie, Loralyn, 2016

were married in 1984. More about me in Book III

My parents had professional pictures taken every year by a gentleman named Hans Roth. We all loved him. He would come to the house and pick a spot for the pictures. With six acres of oak trees and landscaping, he was never wanting for a fabulous backdrop. My father would write a poem for the card summing up the happenings of the year for the family. Here are some samples of the cards over the years.

Marsha, Loralyn, Valerie, 1950

Valerie, Loralyn, Baby Charise, Marsha, 1952

Charise, Marsha, Valerie, Loralyn, Lucille, Marshal, 1954

1956

John, Marshal, Loralyn, Lucille, Valerie, Charise, Marsha 1961

Charise, Marsha, Valerie, Loralyn 1966

John Michael, Loralyn, David, Charise, Marsha, Allen, 1967

Marshal, Lucille, John W. Charise, Marsha, Allen L, Loralyn, Kevin W., Valerie, David W. W. = Wagner, L= Litke, 1969

Marsha, John, Loralyn, Kevin, Charise, Valerie, David 1970

Bud, Byron W., Charise, Jack L., Marsha, Allen L., Dobie G., Valyrie G., Valerie, Paul W., Kevin W. Loralyn, David W., John Michael W., 1976
(W.=Werner, G=Gillum, L=Litke, W=Wagner)

Hans Roth front left, photographer

CHAPTER 9
THE RANCH - VALOMALUMA CHALET

In 1948, my parents bought a beautiful piece of property outside Mariposa, CA that the family still owns today. My father had lived through two world wars and was determined to have some place to take his family in case of another war. This was an ideal location to be able to live off the grid, with water, a large "victory" garden, and farm animals. There was even a wood burning stove for heat, kerosene lanterns throughout, an indoor spring, and a wood burning cooking stove. It is 23 acres with several pastures, and on the Middle Fork of the Chowchilla River. The main house consisted of a dining room, kitchen, living room, master bedroom, bathroom, and a cute little attic bedroom. The kitchen had a pantry with an indoor spring, something you don't see every day. There was gravity flow water to the house from one of the six springs on the property.

Valoma Luma Chalet, Ranch

My parents named the property Valomaluma. The "Va" stood for Valerie (5), their second daughter, the "lo" was for Loralyn (7), their eldest daughter, and the "ma" for Marsha (3), their youngest. The "lu" was for Lucille and the "ma" for Marshal. That name stood for four years until 1952 when I was born. They had to think of something to include this new surprise package. They added Chalet, the "Ch" for Charise, and "Hale" stood between the "C" and the "T"! I've always thought that was so clever. We still call the "Ranch" Valomaluma Chalet to this day as the 4th generation uses this wonderful house and property.

My father immediately set out to add a bedroom with, Abe Block. Abe was the carpenter for the Hale Stores and a great friend of dad's. It is more like a porch because the windows come out in the summer and it resembles a screened in porch. There are 4 closets with mirrors in stair steps that still represent the four girl's heights so many years ago.

Marsha, Loralyn, Valerie, Charise Fancy Pants, 1956.

Early on a spring holding tank was dug and a pump house was built to provide a better process for delivering water. Not being a full-time residence, we could not raise chickens, but did have guests throughout the summer, so the chicken house became a two bedroom, one bath guest house, but keeping "every man's dream" workshop next to it. My mother had an outside washing machine and would hang all the clothes on a clothes line to dry. They had goats the first ten years or so, and my father would load them in the back of his Cadillac sedan to take them to the neighbors each Labor Day for the winter. When that got a bit much for just the summer, my dad and sisters changed the Goat House into a teenage rumpus room of sorts. It had one bath, a kitchenette, with two twin beds against the outside walls that acted as couches. Adding a phonograph record player was all that was needed.

My parents built a swimming pool in 1952. A big, 40x20 foot pool. Only engineering flaw was that my father thought it a good idea to build it over a spring, which to this day has caused us problems with cracks causing water and willows to push up through the bottom. Cleaning that pool for summer was a putrid job, often having to shovel dead animals out of the deep end.

Hale Girls with Chief Lemi, last chief of the Miwok Indians, 1955.

Twice we found a grown deer. We would scrub the algae off the walls and bottom and hose everything down. It took all of us a full day to get it clean.

When we would get to the ranch on the day after school closed there was dead grass everywhere. This had to be mowed and some of it my father would "Control Burn", then we would have to rake all the soot back and forth until it was dirt again. We all hated that job until one day he was "control burning" while the firemen were up at the little old lady's property next door doing the same thing. The firemen were sitting on a big rock overlooking the Ranch while taking a break when our fire got away from my father and lit up the peach and apple trees right behind the house like a Christmas tree. I still remember the firemen laughing so hard they almost fell off the rock!

It would take 2 weeks to fill the pool and by the time 4th of July came along, it was only 2/3 full, but we didn't care at that point, we would swim in it anyway and invited our friends to as well. It was not heated, but with high ninety-degree weather, who cared? At night, it was like a bath tub after the sun had been beating on it all day. And that brings me to the night we almost always went swimming.

My family would host a 4th of July party complete with fireworks and sparklers for all. They invited the whole town with an ad in the Mariposa Gazette. The longest operating newspaper in the state of California to this day, by the way. My father learned to put on quite a fireworks show, and the USONA fire department would come with the engine and enjoy the festivities, just in case we would need them. My mother would read the Declaration of Independence in her theatrical voice and the audience would be spellbound. There were hot dogs and hamburgers, watermelon, numerous desserts, beer, Koolaid, and of course roasted marshmallows. It was always one of the funnest days of the year for me. We continue that tradition to this day at our Tahoe house.

A point of interest: our road, a very long road going from Hwy 49 to Indian Peak, was named USONA. Pathfinder John C. Fremont wanted to change the name of the U.S.A. to the United States of North America because there was a South America. He asked his father-in-law, Senator Benton, to help. It made it all the way through the House of Representatives, but was turned down in the Senate. There was a small post office at the end of Tip Top Road opposite USONA Road. The entire area was known as USONA. It is, to this day, on every map between Mariposa and Oakhurst on Highway 49. The reason? Because it is capitalized, and the reason it is capitalized is because it stands for United States of North America. But, the map makers don't know that so it is treated as a town in that industry. Now you know an interesting piece of trivia that few people know.

My father bought my oldest sister a retired 10-year-old Hambletonian trotter. Gypsy was the best horse on the planet and taught all of us to ride. I learned by riding on a pillow on her neck before I could walk with Loralyn in the saddle. Then in 1953, we got Lady Lucky, who sprained an ankle in a gopher hole in the meadow some years later, and could only be walked after that. But, Lady Luck turned out to be a great brood mare giving us Magic Star and Mystic Star. Gypsy may have had the record for the oldest Hambletonian, we know she was at least thirty-five when she died. We didn't have her papers to prove it, but she is buried on our neighbor's property along with his old horse, Goldie. That is where our horses stayed when we were not at the Ranch.

We spent Easter week, all summer, and Christmas/New Year's week at the ranch every year until 1964. Then my sister, Marsha married the boy across the road, and my parents didn't approve, so we stopped going and rented it out until I turned 18. That year I went for a visit and came back crying, telling my parents to take it back or sell it, because the current renter was ruining it. We had a family meeting and my sisters and I agreed to keep it up and that is what we did. Treating it as a democracy for decision making and paying $25/month into a kitty in the beginning. We sisters and our husbands are proud of the changes and improvements we have made to the ranch, always keeping the original charm. Keeping the property cut and cleared is a constant battle, but keeping horses and cattle in the pastures over the years have been a big help. My parents succumbed to a telephone in 1962, a party line, and we put in internet around 2008, but still no TV. We have a trash compactor, but still no dishwasher or garbage disposal. The heat is still provided by a central wood burning stove and space heaters. But, the house is very comfortable, and we in no way are "roughing it." Polished half logs and Indian rugs decorate the inside, an it is quaint and homey to all generations.

Middle fork of the Chowchilla River

You can't explain the charm of the place to anyone unless they have been there. It is indeed a piece of paradise on earth and we all feel that way about it. We are passing that love down to the 4th generation and have formed an LLC to protect it. We are so proud watching our children carry on that democracy and making decisions together with their cousins. From what we are seeing, the Ranch is in good hands, and it is wonderful the way the families work together.

Ranch Wishes

It is this generation's wish that the Ranch always be cared for and loved, and passed down through the family. Share it with your spouses, but will it to your children. It is a very special place for us all.

CHAPTER 10
BOHEMIAN CLUB AND GROVE

The Theatre at the Bohemian Club on Taylor St., San Francisco

The Bohemian Club, located on Taylor Street in San Francisco, was founded by a group of artists, writers, lawyers, and actors in 1872. All were male, many were journalists who wrote for the San Francisco Examiner. I'm not sure when my grandfather and his two brothers, Reuben Brooks and Prentis Cobb Hale joined, but I would imagine in the 1890s. I know my father got his acceptance letter on July 7, 1925 at the age of twenty-two. The Grove is located on the Russian River near Monte Rio.

Grove Main Stage

It is an unbelievable property with giant redwoods, a lake, and rather steep hills rising from the main floor. There are numerous camps throughout the forest and no permanent structures, other than the outdoor dining room kitchen, are allowed.

All members belong to a camp. There are "working" camps such as Aviary and Tunerville. These members donate a certain amount of time to singing and playing instruments both at the Grove and at the club on Taylor Street in San Francisco. The Bohemian Club has always been expensive and exclusive. The Grove was selected as the secret location during World War II when discussions regarding the Atom bomb were needed. Because it was impossible to plant listening devices, or penetrate without being detected, the government men and scientists gathered at the Russian River location amongst the redwood trees in the huge open aired outdoor dining room and the fateful decision was made. I went through grade school with a boy whose parents were friends with the man who dropped the bomb over Hiroshima. He wasn't supposed to tell me but he was my best friend and grade school "boyfriend", so he did. I think the man later committed suicide, but I know he was haunted the rest of his life.

Bohemian Grove Fireside Chat

My father was a member of Dragons Camp. Just a little bit in from the main entrance and up on the left. There are no solid structures in any of the camps accept the bathrooms. There are open "manger" type bars and barracks. Most living is done outdoors including a magnificent dining room located on the redwood grove floor near the stage and lake. My father's campmates were all good friends and we called many of them "uncle". There was Augie Augustine, Art Linkletter, Walt Disney, Hernando Courtright, Dennis Day, Bob Evans, Carl Hague, Edgar Bergen, etc. Other than Edgar, Art and Dennis, I really didn't know what the others did.

Bottom row: second in: Dennis Day, Hernando Courtright, Art Linkletter
Second Row Right Side: Edgar Bergen, Marshal Hale

Occupations were not discussed in my fathers' day. They went to the club and the two-week encampment (last two weeks of July) to get away from the pressures of their professional lives. They did not discuss business and wheel and deal. It just wasn't accepted.

When I went to Los Angeles with my mother to tour some of her former movie studios I learned that Hernando Courtwright owned the Beverly Wilshire and half of Wilshire Blvd. I would expect you all to know who Walt Disney was, but you may not remember Dennis Day or Art Linkletter. Art had a show on television, "People Are Funny" for many years, and was a very witty and funny guy. One of the segments was where he would ask little kids questions. It was titled "Kids Say The Darndest Things" and some of the answers were hysterical. Dennis Day was an Irish tenor and side kick to Jack Benny (Google Jack Benny) on Jack's variety show. There is still no one on earth that can sing "Danny Boy" like Dennis. He had ten kids and lived in the San Fernando Valley. Mom and I visited him when I was twelve on our Hollywood trip, and to this day I remember the house, his pretty wife, Peggy, the pool, and all the kids. Good Irish Catholic family, but evidently, they ran out of names because two of the girls were named Mary Margaret and Margaret Mary.

Bohemian set on Main Stage

My father was, I realize now, the last of the Renaissance men. He sang, danced, was an accomplished athlete, he was a fair carpenter, an excellent landscape architect, and a writer and poet. However, he could not cook. I know for a fact he didn't know how to turn on the stove or oven. The Grove was made for his talents. There are two plays during the encampment. The High Jinx, which is a drama, and the Low Jinx, which is a comedy. All parts are played by men. Yes, we have pictures of my father as a woman. He was not pretty. The sides of the main stage are flanked by magnificent redwoods and the backdrop to the stage is a steep hill with a fern lined zig zag path rising about 100 feet up behind the stage. There are redwoods on either side of the rise making a breathtaking backdrop.

It was in one of the High Jinx productions that my father danced for the Prince of Sweden, later to become King, Gustaf VI Adolf. The prince complimented my father on his magnificent performance. Other High Jinx productions were "Truth", "The Golden Feather", 1939 and "Tetecan" in 1950. But, my father also did many of the Low Jinx, comedies. "Vienna Roll", "Virgin Ore or The Assayer's Dream", "The Bee Keeper's Supplies, or Why Go Elsewhere to Get Stung," and the "Gay Nighties"! Obviously, they all had double meanings and were filled with very funny, clever lines. He would come home and practice his lines with me so that by the time he went off to the Grove, I knew every line and couldn't wait to hear the report of what really went on, and how far they deviated from the script. One was called "The Jockey's Trap, or The Horses Behind". Obviously, one can see the double entendre here. In this one there were three devious bankers trying to take advantage of the main character. My dad played one banker (he served on the board of Bank of America), the second was Rudy Petersen, the president of Bank of America at the time, and the third was the president of United California Bank (I can't remember his name). They were all dressed up as Melodrama characters with waxed mustaches, top hats, and all. I remember the three of them sang a song that has the lines; "We're dastardly, despicable, depraved!!!..... three dirty bankers...." I still remember the tune. It was hilarious. Members like Dan Rowen and Dick Martin also joined into the fun. I could recite their entire routine for years because my father took notes for me.

Cremation of Care

The encampment (last two weeks of July) opens with the Cremation of Care. There is a beautiful lake with a large stone carved owl (the club mascot) at one end. This is where people get the idea it is a cult. No, folks, it is not, but the ceremony, which I have never seen first-hand since women are not allowed in the camp except to the picnics, is very ceremonial complete with hooded capes. All the members sit on the grass around the lake, but there are a few Redwood half log benches. These are reserved for the "Old Guard", men who have been members for 40 years. My father, having joined at 22, was the youngest of the Old Guard and had that privilege for many years. One year a gentleman tapped my father's shoulder and said, "Excuse me, Sir, is it okay if I sit at your feet here?" My father said, "Oh, yes, by all means." It was former President Gerald Ford. Being the mere President of the United States gets you nowhere at the Grove.

And, speaking of such, it was an unwritten rule that no sitting president would attend the Grove while in office. It is just too disruptive to what the grove is all about. President Herbert Hoover, for example, never attended while in office. President Richard Nixon, however, wanted to and was told "NO" by the Bohemian Board of Directors. It is a huge privilege to be invited by a member to attend, and it is not easily arranged. He took Conrad Hilton and my mother's cousin Joshua Bryant Powers.

Bohemian mascot, Owl by the lake

There are Fireside Chats every year that would blow your socks off. People like George Schultz while he was Secretary of State was a speaker. Scientists were often the most fascinating. I remember my father coming home about 1964 and telling us that satellites would be able to tell you what was wrong with a car that had its hood up on the side of the road, from space. There were other predictions that have all come true and a few that are still a few years away, even though these talks were more than 40 years ago.

Although I often attended parties and plays at the main club in San Francisco, each year I looked forward to going to the Spring Picnic at the Grove. It was the one time that ladies were invited into the Grove and there was the most amazing entertainment put on at Tunerville or one of the stages. One year, I was getting out of my car with my fiancé, Bud Werner, when Edgar Bergen recognized me. Now, for those of you too young to remember, other than being Candice Bergen's father, Edgar was the most famous ventriloquist in the world. He held that distinction for many many years. He was on the Jack Benny Show, The Ed Sullivan Show, The Carol Burnett Show, and every variety show on TV. He did Vegas, New York, and all the world stages. He got his start in Vaudeville. So, in the parking lot, he said to me, "You're Marshal's daughter, aren't you?" I said, "Yes, Mr. Bergen, I am, I'm Charise, and this is my fiancé, Bud Werner." Edgar said, "Then you are going up to Dragons Camp?" And, of course I said, "Yes." He asked Bud if he could carry a large suitcase for him, and Bud agreed. As we were walking along ahead, I said to Bud, "For God's sake don't drop it, you are carrying a million dollars in there. I wasn't sure if it was Charlie McCarthy or Mortimer Snerd, but I knew what they were insured for! These were the most famous puppets in the world and probably still are. Generations could still name them today.

You have heard many stories about the Grove and shenanigans that may or may not have gone on. I am sure many of the stories are true, but my father maintained until the day he died, he never saw a woman in the encampment. If the men wanted that sort of entertainment, there were places to go in Monte Rio, and rumor has it they multiplied greatly for those last two weeks in July. We were privy to the kind of fun grown men can have acting like little boys especially when money is no object. Aside from never seeing a tree that hadn't been peed on at one time or another, these men stayed up all hours drinking and telling stories, and sometimes decided on an adventure like this one, that is truly a story to rival Dean Martin, Frank Sinatra and the rest of The Rat Pack. One night a group of Dragon members were sitting around the campfire in the wee hours of the morning and one of them asks where is Dennis Day? Another says, "Oh, he's opening in Vegas on Saturday so he is there rehearsing." Another says, "Really? We should go see how the rehearsal is going, I love his act." Hernando Courtright says, "Well, I have my plane." So, a group of them, my father included, decide this is a fine idea. After making a phone call to the pilot, they go meet him at the private air strip. Now, none of them had the foresight to change their clothing. They land in Las Vegas, have a taxi waiting, at 9:30AM, this pack of Bohemians, I think there were five of them, go walking into The Sands Hotel wearing their pajamas, robes, and slippers. Their scotches, of course, are still in hand, and into the showroom they go and sit down at one of the tables. Dennis looks up and one of them yells, "Dennis, your good buddies have flown down to critique your rehearsal!" You can't make this stuff up!!

During WWII, they held Bohemian events at Tiptoe Lane (our home) because of the gas rationing. And, in 1975 my parents had a big Bohemian party at the house. Art Linkletter performed "Bad, Bad, Leroy Brown" and brought down the house. There was a piano set up in the back yard on a rise that became a make shift stage, and chairs for the audience. Like the Grove stage, this one had a backdrop of Live Oak trees, ferns, camellias and beautiful rocks gong up a hill. There was singing, dancing, and a lot of joke telling! Bohemian entertainment is unparalleled.   I remember it was in late October, because Carl Hague came up to me in the shoulder to shoulder cocktail crowd and asked when I was going to start a family. I looked down at my very large stomach and said, "Jeez, Carl, I don't know, maybe in about a month!" Byron was born Nov. 30th!

Another funny story; a couple of years before Daddy died, he took me to the club one evening to see some entertainment on a "Ladies Night". I was about thirty-five at the time. A young man about my age, or a little older, came up to me and started talking to me while we were having cocktails and appetizers. I suddenly realized that he assumed I was Dad's wife. I was wearing my wedding ring. My father was standing over my right shoulder talking to a friend. I soon realized this man was arrogant and rude, and then he said something like, "Is it really worth it, why would you be with such an old man?" Never taking my eyes off him, I said, "Well, why don't you ask him? Daddy, this young man wants to ask you a question." He turned three shades of red, and said, "Oh, sorry, Sir, it was just a misunderstanding." I then turned and joined my father.

CHAPTER 11
WHIMSEY RUNS IN THE FAMILY

I've learned a lot this year just past
And I can walk around at last.
It keeps me out one step ahead
Until I'm shuffled off to bed.

I have my Aunties buffaloed
Cause they don't always know I knowed
And as for Grandma - tra - la - la
An easy push, and so's Grandpa.

But Mommy and my Daddy too
Are getting wise to what I do
And though they treat me like a man
I'm thinking 'bout a cross-up plan.

Though not 'til after Christmas time
Right now I'm going to keep in line
So here's a greeting bright and fair
From all our family, everywhere.

John Michael Wagner

Charise, Lucille and Marshal Hale
Loralyn, Valerie and Marsha, too

Inside of 1965 Christmas card

My father had a very whimsical sense of humor and loved whimsical art. My sister, Valerie and I share that. Slipknot, was our family ghost. Every family should have one. When we did something wrong, we would blame it on Slipknot! When we couldn't find something, then, Slipknot took it. He moved with us from our house to the Ranch and then to our houses when we left home, and I think he is on his 4th generation of taking care of the Hale Family now. He even became our "safe" word, because who else on earth would know his name! My father loved elves, Leprechauns, and "the little people"! My parents added on a family room in 1957 to the house on Tiptoe Lane, and in this completely round addition, with a bathroom literally behind the fireplace, my father had a mural commissioned. Since we lived in a real life oak tree forest with ferns and lush ground cover, the mural was of elves living in a forest. One sat on top of a very tall mushroom. Dad told us that the little elf fell asleep and the mushroom grew so tall that he couldn't get down!

We had a dog named Wiggles and a cat named Fancy Pants. Our nicknames were Pride and Joy (Loralyn), Honey Bunch (Valerie), Sweetheart Darling (Marsha), and Honey Bun (Charise). He wrote poems and stories of castles and dragons and some very whimsical characters. Every year, my father would meet with good friend Janice Rossi, and they would compose the poems for our Christmas cards. They were clever and funny, and told the story of what had happened in our family over the past year. My favorite was when my oldest nephew, John Michael, was one and a half, and they wrote it as if he was telling the story.

I have it memorized.
"I've learned a lot this year just past,
And I can walk around at last!
It keeps me just a step ahead,
Until I'm shuffled off to bed. I keep my aunties buffaloed
Cuz they don't always know I knowed!
As for Grandma – tra-la-la
An easy push, and so's grandpa. But, Mommy and my Daddy too

Are getting wise to what I do.
And though they treat me like a man
I'm thinking 'bout a cross-up plan. Though not 'til after Christmas time
Right now I'm going to keep in line
So, here's a greeting bright and far
From all our family, everywhere."

Dad loved Edgar Allan Poe, and could recite "The Raven" by memory. He, also, could recite a little-known poem by Lewis Caroll, "Phantasmagoria." It became my favorite poem, and I can still recite the first part. It is about a little ghost, of course. Look it up, it is clever and sweet, and thoroughly entertaining.

Dad's favorite cartoon was Prince Valiant. He never missed the Sunday comics. He would tell me stories of little people in the forest, but could also have a wicked and mischievous sense of humor. You'll see that a bit later while we were traveling with Jack, my husband.

CHAPTER 12
TRAVELING

Lucille and Marshal loved to travel. The first trip I can remember is going to **Disneyland** in 1957. I was five years old, and of course, we didn't exactly get the normal treatment since Walt Disney was a campmate of my fathers at the Bohemian Grove. We checked into the Disneyland Hotel, which in those days

was quite a distance away from the park with nothing in-between. We took the car to the main entrance where Walt met us and escorted us down Main Street and into the park. He spent most of the afternoon with us as we went on the rides and got a firsthand account how each one came about. Can you imagine the excitement in his voice as he described his vision and how it came to fruition? A truly unique experience that I will never forget. It made such an impression on me that I still remember today sitting in Mythology class as a high school freshman on a sunny December afternoon when I learned Walt Disney had died. My eyes filled with tears of sadness that this great man was no longer with us.

It was on this trip that I met my father's first wife, Helen. We were having dinner at the hotel, and they sat me in a high chair at the end of the table. I can picture the dining room and where everyone was sitting. I remember having my Donald Duck hat in my lap since I wasn't allowed to wear it at the table. Everyone else wanted a Mickey Mouse hat, but I wanted the Donald Duck, complete with yellow bill and all. I also remember my father saying, "So, Helen, we'll put you next to the baby and see what kind of mother you would have made." I didn't realize there was anything wrong with saying that until I looked at my mother's face; if looks could kill, I

am sure my father would have been dead on the spot! Helen seemed to take it in stride, however, as memory serves me.

When I was six, they took the family to Hawaii for the first time. We stayed in a

Loralyn, Valerie, Marsha, and Charise, 1957

cottage at the Halekulani Hotel on Waikiki Beach. A beautiful, Hawaiian garden hotel with the flavor of old Hawaii. We fell in love with the islands. The music, the hula, the ocean, what was not to like? We would have many vacations at the Halekulani in the future.

There were many trips in which they took me. I was born a month before my father was fifty, and two months before my mother was forty-one. When they decided, they wanted to travel, it was easier to take me along. Those trips will be covered in Book III.

1962, my parents traveled to the **Caribbean** and toured all the islands. They went alone on this trip; I was in the fourth grade and had multiplication and division to learn.

In 1967, my parents went to **Yugoslavia and the USSR**. I remember my mother saying she would probably never eat peas and carrots again. They had them every night as a vegetable while in Russia. And, the country must have gotten a bargain on royal blue fabric, because she said everyone wore it. Again, lessons in freedom and free trade.

Then, as I was in college, and married in 1973, my parents began to take their grandsons on trips until my mother passed away in 1981. They took them to **Europe, Australia and New Zealand** .

In 1981, my mother got throat cancer and after her treatment, embarked on a trip with my father and youngest nephew, Paul Wagner. They had to cut the trip short and bring my mother home. The cancer had gone to her brain and once they started her on fluids, it put too much pressure on her brain, and she passed away the following night on September 11, 1981. One of my biggest disappointments was that my mother didn't get to meet my husband, Jack McHugh. The Irish lad and lassie would have gotten along famously, I know!

My father then took Loralyn and Johnny on a trip to Europe, and later me and Jack. I'll cover our trip in the Charise and Jack chapter.

PART III

CHARISE

CHAPTER 13
CHARISE

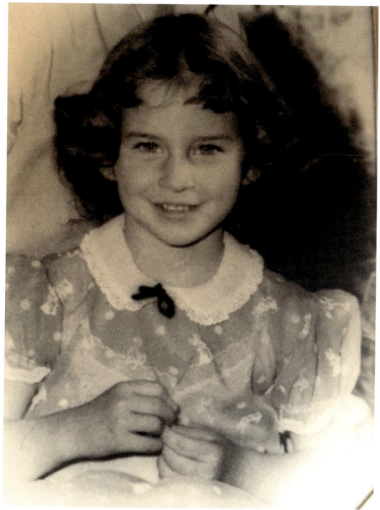

Charise Hale Werner McHugh (9/23/1952-)

I was the fourth daughter born to Lucille and Marshal. Lucille was almost forty-one and Marshal almost fifty when I arrived on September 23,1952. My parents were watching "Scaramouch", a movie at the Broadway Movie Theater in Burlingame, California when my mother went into labor. I was born at Mills Memorial Hospital in San Mateo on a Tuesday at 12:26am. I was born breech, feet first, and face up. Should have known right then that I would have a mind of my own! I was also born with my arms over my head. In the delivery, my left arm was broken, and I wore a tiny little cast for six weeks. There was an eight-year gap between myself and my next sister, Marsha. I was a Tom Boy and loved climbing trees and making tree forts on the six acres in Hillsborough and riding horses, fishing, and swimming at the Ranch. I was hit by a car when I was five. My sisters were at the orthodontist on Cappuccino in Burlingame, and my sister, Loralyn, crossed the street to the car. I wanted to go with her. She told me to stay, but I didn't listen, and crossed anyway. The car broke my right collar bone, and I was taken to the hospital in a police car, with my stick horse preventing the door from closing all the way for the ride. My sister, Valerie held it closed, while my mother held me in her arms in the back seat. I was a very friendly child, so my first-grade teacher, Mrs. Fisher, was so afraid I would get in a car with a stranger, that she asked my mother to come to school so they could talk to me and caution me about strangers.

I attended North Hillsborough Elementary School, William H. Crocker Intermediate School, both in Hillsborough, and then Castilleja High School for Girls in Palo Alto.

I also took eight years of tap, acrobatics, and Modern Jazz at Les Williams Dance Studio from Les Williams. He was an important influence in my life and I loved him dearly. I did the eulogy at his funeral in April of 2015. He was a Tuskegee Airman and was taught dance by Bo Jangles. Wonderful, proud, talented man.

Leslie A. Williams
(1920-2015)

I will tell about all the traveling I did as a child in the next chapter. Forty-eight countries by the time I was seventeen. That, and the fact that I often had to take care of my parents at a very young age, were probably the two factors that most shaped the person I am.

Since there are several pictures of me in this book, I should mention that I had my nose done when I was fourteen. I had a very large nose, one that did not match the rest of my features. Being a Hale trait, my father offered, and at the age of twelve, I said, "Oh, no Daddy, I like my nose." Two years later, not so much! I had an excellent doctor, Dr. Harry Buncke, who in 1970

Charise, age 13

became quite famous for being the doctor that transferred a doctor's toes to his hand after he lost all his fingers in the big earthquake in Mexico City. He took out the large bump in my nose, and raised the tip from 90 degrees to 120. Probably, more information than you needed to know, but I found it very interesting. I was fourteen and had stopped growing, a prerequisite. I am sad to say that it did have a big impact on my life. I had been teased as a child by my peers unmercifully. I have a lot of empathy for kids who are bullied. I can tell you, it was no fun. I can also tell you, that because of that experience, I have never bullied or criticized anyone for their appearance. It is very hurtful.

In my 8th grade yearbook, Kathy Murr wrote, "Roses are red, violets are blue, and you have a nose like a B-52." All I could think of was that I could never say that to someone who was my friend, and I also thought, yours is almost as big as mine, but said nothing back! It was also amazing how boys suddenly noticed me. I have always been supportive of anyone who decided on plastic surgery, within reason, of course. I say, if it makes you feel better about yourself, and you can afford it, and it is not dangerous, go for it. Don't make a habit of it, aging gracefully is more attractive. Just my opinion. But, life is too short to be unhappy with yourself if it's something you can change.

Another thing that had a big impact on my life, is that my parents were both binge drinkers. They could go months without drinking a drop, but when one would start, the other would follow, and it would be days before they sobered up, usually, not without help. It's a lot of responsibility on a nine-year-old (my sisters were already married or out of the house at school) to order liquor to be delivered by a cab and pay for it (that wouldn't happen today), or to arrange for the ambulance to have them carted off to a hospital or sanitarium. I knew exactly when the time was right and usually coordinated both of them at the same time. Sometimes this was with the help of our family doctor, but sometimes not. I had to assess the situation and move quickly or the window would close.

I know my sisters had a very different childhood than mine and that some of my book may be hard for them to read. I think it was a very ridged household and my father didn't show much affection. Maybe my parents realized they were too tough on them, or maybe my parents were tired by the time they had me? Or maybe because it was like I was an only child with the age difference between me and my sisters. I know they were very proud of Valerie and Loralyn. They would brag about them, and tell me all the time about what they were doing.

My fondest memories were when I was traveling with my parents or at the Ranch because they never drank then. And, my mother stopped drinking when I was twelve, so I had more of my childhood without her ever taking a drink. I think she did give up drinking for me because I was considering moving up to Santa Rosa with

Loralyn, and she would lose me. I thank Loralyn again for the role she played in my childhood.

As a result, of their drinking, I am a pleaser. I want to please all the people, all the time. That's one reason I was such a successful Chamber of Commerce executive.

My parents were both brilliant and taught me so many things. My mother took a radical treatment for alcohol abuse and never had a drink again. I admire her greatly for that. My father would still go on the occasional binge, and I taught my mother how to time the ambulance so he would be ready and go willingly. Well, maybe not willingly, but we could make it happen. It wasn't until my father met my husband, Jack, that I saw him go out for a night on the town to the Bohemian Club and come back and not drink the next day. Jack taught me the difference between social drinking and alcoholic drinking. The last couple of years of my father's life, I learned not to panic if he had a drink and was able to enjoy an evening with him when he had a cocktail. Maybe not completely relaxed, but enjoyed it just the same.

When I was sixteen, I locked myself out of my car on Broadway Ave. in Burlingame. The Wells Fargo Bank was across the street and just as I was going to cross and ask if I could use their phone, a man stepped out of the bank and crossed to his car parked next to mine. He saw the agitated look on my face, and said "Are you okay, do you need help?" As I looked up to those famous blue eyes, I said, "Oh, Mr. Crosby, I locked my keys in the car." He said, "Do you live nearby? I could take you to get a spare set." I said to Bing, "Really? Yes, I live in Hillsborough, but a little further up the hill than you." (Everyone knew where Bing Crosby lived. He had moved his family to Hillsborough just a few years prior.) I got in his car, and he drove me home to get my keys and then drove me back to Broadway. Another wonderful gentleman!

CHAPTER 14
TRAVELING WITH MY PARENTS

My mother took incredible pictures on all our travels. But, she took slides and they were all in carousels. She often showed them at schools and assemblies, because along with her diaries, she could recreate history. However, there were about 50 carousels, and in 2010, I decided I just couldn't keep them. I should have. So, you will not see many personal pictures associated with many of these trips. I do have her diaries.

In 1961, my parents decided to take a three and half month trip to Europe and took me with them. The schools figured I would get a much better education traveling through Europe than in a classroom, so armed with an English book and Math book, off we went. We sailed from New York on the USS United States, the fasted luxury liner in the world at the time, and arrived at La Havre, France on April 14th. We traveled through France, Germany, Hungary, Austria, Liechtenstein, Switzerland, Italy, Portugal, Holland, Denmark, Sweden, and England. I wore only dresses, not slacks, wasn't allowed to chew gum, and had to curtsy when introduced. My mother was determined to show the Europeans, that not all Americans were "Ugly Americans" with no manners. This was only fifteen years after the end of WWII so the bombed-out buildings were still numerous and emotions were still volatile. We were in East Berlin six weeks before the wall went up. At eight, I can tell you the oppression of an eastern block country was not lost on me. I couldn't wait to get back to West Berlin. I feared all the soldiers with machine guns. I was scared that I might step on the lawn and be shot because there were signs to not walk on the grass. In 1961, almost nothing had been rebuilt in East Germany. There were facades, like movie set fronts on the main boulevard to look like modern buildings, but our driver and guide took us on the next street over and we could see the lumber holding up the fronts. People were gathered in front of a store window looking at the "new" black and white television sets.

Madurodam, The Hague, Holland

I spent a day and evening in East Berlin with Oscar Blum's brother, his wife and daughter. Isolde was about 18, later she became a doctor. I couldn't fathom how they could live under those conditions. And, talk about drab. No flowers, little landscaping, and everything was painted gray or brown. The clothes were colorless. Hungary was the same way, but at least they had the cute storks nesting on the chimneys! I have always said that all Americans should have that experience. You have no idea what freedom is until you lose it, even for a few hours.

When I was introduced to the manager of the hotel in Copenhagen, after being in Germany and Austria for weeks, I said "Danke sehr" (thank you very much in German) as I curtsied. He visibly bristled, and said you are not in Germany, you are in Denmark now!" He then gave me the proper Danish word for thank you. My mother had to explain why he was so upset. The wounds were still raw with the German occupation just fifteen years prior. I loved Denmark and, of course, seeing where Hans Christian Andersen was born and Tivoli Park were definite highlights. But, Holland was my favorite country, probably because of Madurodam in The Hague. A complete miniature city of 1:25 scale models of buildings, houses, farms, planes, trains, and ships in the canals. It is on about an acre and is absolutely incredible.

My mother kept a diary of everything. And, I do mean everything. She wrote copious notes of the history the guide would tell us every day and after my father and I went to bed or at 5am in the morning she would sit on the toilet seat in the bathroom, so not to disturb us, and write. She went through three volumes on this trip! We had a car and driver, so we went at our own pace, but most days were very full. My parents loved history.

My father carried a note in his wallet, which I still have, that had every king of England from Egbert to Elizabeth. He said it was his guide as to when things were happening in comparison to who was on the British throne. It put history into perspective for him. There was not a cathedral or museum that was missed, I can assure you. While in a museum in Florence, I looked up and exclaimed, "Oh, no, not another Peter Paul Reuben's!" Coming out of an eight-year old's mouth it was pretty funny. My mother traveled with gum and lifesavers and would be surrounded by children as she passed them out. I particularly remember standing in front of the house where Christopher Columbus was born in Genoa, and not being sure my mother would ever be able to release herself from the children. That same day we visited the ancient ruins of Pompeii. Not until we visited Egypt a few years later would I be as impressed with how advanced ancient civilizations were. They had running water delivered to each house via stone aqueducts! Just amazing. Obviously, I am only touching on a few highlights of an incredible three and a half months!

Arundel Castle, my father's favorite

Versailles

The movie "Gigi" came out that year, and since we were traveling off season, I was often the only child in the hotel or restaurant. So, almost every night we were serenaded with Maurice Chevalier's "Thank Heaven for Little Girls." My father and I would dance to it and it became our song. We danced to it at my wedding.

At the end of our trip we met my sisters, Valerie and Marsha, who had been on tour with their high school, in London in time for July 4th! I don't recommend celebrating it in England, for some reason, they just don't get it.

In 1963, they again took me and Marsha out of school in April, and we spent six weeks in **Asia**. We traveled extensively through Japan, then Taiwan, Macao, Thailand, and Hong Kong. On this trip, we were inundated with temples and shrines. The history and culture was amazing. Again, what we learned could not be taught in a classroom. When I got back, I wrote a term paper on Japan and got an "A". One of the things that struck me the most was the space or lack thereof. Every hillside,

5 Flies restaurant founded in 1627 in Amsterdam

Shakespeare Country

and tiny patch of land was planted or utilized. The only open space was Nikko National Park outside of Tokyo. We went to Osaka, Kobe, Takamatsu, and Hiroshima. The museum in Hiroshima was, of course, horrible and graphic. Something I hope the world never experiences again. It was an incredible trip learning about cultures so different from our own.

My parents always made sure we got out into the country every place we visited so we could see how the natives of that land lived. We visited local inns, restaurants, markets, and parks. In each country, we often visited department stores since that was my father's vocation, but also hospitals since he was on the board of one, as well as a Bank of America. We were entertained by the manager of the local Bank of America many times and visited their homes and family. I will tell you a couple of stories on this later.

My sixth-grade year we went to **Mexico and Central America**; Mexico, Guatemala, and El Salvador. Valerie came along on this trip, and we went in December. We spent Christmas in Oaxaca and New Years in San Salvador. There was no problem locating my mother in a crowd in either country. My mother was 5'7" and very blonde. She would be a head taller than any native and that blonde hair was hard to miss. Children would gather around her and want to touch her hair.

A few months prior to the trip, my father reconnected with Alfredo Mejia. Alfredo was on the 1924 Olympic swim team for El Salvador. My father called him on the telephone after forty years. He and his Canadian wife, Helen, insisted we stay with them at their plantation. I have

Charise, 1969 Panama Canal

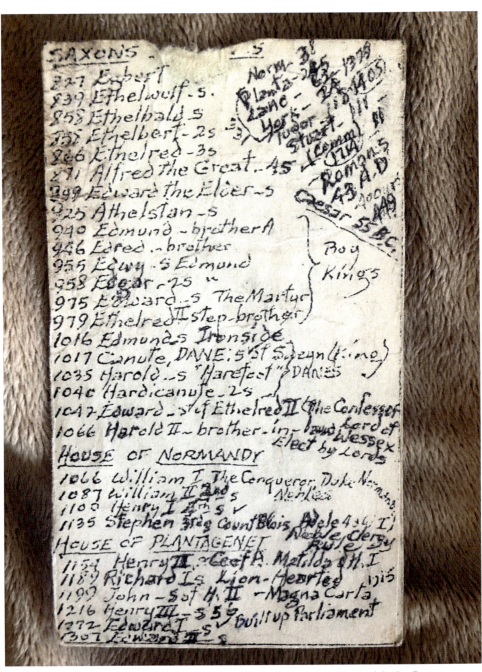

My father's guide, the British monarchy by House, starting with the Saxons

1327 Edward III — (Black Prince)
1377 Richard II grandson Longbow
HOUSE OF LANCASTER Red
1399 Henry IV grandson E III 1337-1453
1413 Henry V s Hundred Years
1422 Henry VI s (White) Jean of Arc
HOUSE OF YORK (Plantagenet)
1461 Edward IV s Duke York descends E III
1483 Edward V s
1483 Richard III brother E IV mother
HOUSE OF TUDOR Tower A s E III
1485 Henry VII s Taxation Amer. discov.
1509 Henry VIII s
1547 Edward VI s Church of England
1553 Mary d H VIII Catholic
1558 Elizabeth d H VIII Ch. of Eng. re-estb.
HOUSE OF STUART
1603 James I s of Mary and James VI of Scot.
1625 Charles I s Struggle with Parliment
COMMONWEALTH (Puritans)
1649 — Council of State — Gov't by Parliment
1653 — Protectorate of Oliver Cromwell
1658 — " Richard Cromwell 1659 — Parliment
HOUSE OF STUART
1660 Charles II s C I (Restored)
1685 James II — brother C II Catholic
1689 Mary II d W of Orange (Parliment Fled to Fr. invite)
1702 Anne — sister (Duke M of s invite) Gibraltar
HOUSE OF HANOVER (Gibraltar)
1714 George I Anne's 2nd cousin France
1721 George II — 7 years War
1760 George III — grandson — Revolution World naval
1820 George IV s power
1836 Will 4th Jr.
1837 Victoria granddaughter Geo III
SAXE-COBURG Edward VII HANOVER George V

never had better hosts in my entire life. It was unbelievable, the entertaining, meals, the side trips, and their coffee plantation with the sweetest oranges I have ever had to this date. Helen had kitchen staff, cleaning staff, gardeners, and even a woman who did nothing but sew. I remember the seamstress' wages were $2.25 a day! And, they all were head over heels in love with their mistress and her kindness. We fell in love with Helen, Alfredo, and their two daughters and remained friends until they died. If it were not for them, we would not have my niece, Marlena, whom they helped Valerie adopt in 1977.

Charise, Lucille, Marshal 1969 Mazatlan

In the spring of seventh grade, I was once again taken out of school to visit the Middle East; Greece, Turkey, Jordan, Lebanon, Syria, and Egypt. This was perhaps my favorite trip of all, and the one that makes me the saddest. Sad because we loved the people of the Middle East, and it breaks my heart the relationship our countries have today. We took a ship around the Greek isles which was so much fun and steeped in ancient history. When we went to dock in Istanbul, there was a sick passenger, so they were boarding a Turkish doctor. At the last

Charise in Greece with a friend I met there 1965

minute, the Greek crew pulled the ship away from the dock, dumping the Turkish doctor into the brink. The Greek-Turkish Feud was still alive and well after centuries!

As we were checking into our hotel in Beirut, the clerk said, "Oh, you live in Hillsborough? I lived there with a family when I was attending CSM (College of San Mateo)." We just stared at him in disbelief. Might've been the greatest "Small World" story. The Arabic people were very friendly. And, they embraced Western culture in the 1960s. It was not unusual to see Arab men in suits and ties with their scarves on their heads driving around in a convertible Chevrolet.

Island of Crete

Jerusalem was in Jordon back then. You could not visit Israel if you had an Arabic country stamp on your passport, so we did not visit Israel. Jerusalem was wonderful. We were there Easter week, so we walked Christ's walk on Good Friday following the stations of the cross. We went to the Wailing Wall and met a woman who was purported to be 116 years old. We visited the Dead Sea, and I tried my best to go under water and stay there but the salt was just too heavy, and I would pop right back up like a buoy. I was baptized in the Jordon River, where John the Baptist baptized Jesus, by a Catholic archbishop.

One of the most incredible experiences was going to Petra, Jordon. We had to go in on horseback to this ancient city carved out of the sandstone walls. The horses were Arabians, of course, just like we owned at the Ranch at the time. I was damned if I was going to be led on a horse! My father told them I would be fine and to let me ride by myself. We spent the night in a barracks with one other couple and in the morning when my parents planned to hike up the mountain to see the sunrise, I asked if I could stay behind and ask the boy (he was probably my age or a year older) if I could borrow a horse. I did, and he let me. So, here is this 12-year-old American girl riding through the Jordanian countryside, by herself, on horseback, into the ancient sand stone carved "buildings" and out! One of the best and most memorable experiences of my life. Now, fast forward to today! I think it is safe to say that I have a unique experience unknown to another.

We loved Egypt. The pyramids, and how they were built, the Sphinx, the Valley of the Kings, Tutankhamun's tomb, and Abu Simbel Temples up the Aswan River. We were the last boat to see the Abu Simbel temples in their original location, the next week they began moving them 100 feet up so they wouldn't be under water when the Aswan Dam was finished and the canyon flooded to make Lake Nasser. It was also the first time we had ridden on a Hydrofoil, and we were fascinated. There were children on the banks of the river with crocodiles swimming close to shore. I remember how concerned I was when I realized there were no adults in sight!

While in Beirut, we were entertained by the manager of Bank of America and

Marshal. Charise. Lucille. 1970

while the adults went to dinner, I went to a movie with their kids. "The Chalk

Garden," with English subtitles. That was an experience! All these Arab kids watching a Western movie in their own language.

I was reviewing my mother's diary a couple of years ago and she stated. "These Arab people are the kindest, most accommodating race we have ever encountered in all our travels." And, I agree with her. It makes me heartsick to see our relationships with these countries today.

In 1968 and 1969, we spent a week in Mexico, first in Acapulco and the next year a week in Mazatlán. On one of those trips we flew to Panama first to see the canal. An amazing engineering feat! While in Acapulco, we met this lovely family from Mexico and I palled around with their son and daughter who were about my age. We swam during the day in this magnificent pool that had an island in the middle. One evening, they took me to a very exclusive club for disco dancing. There were booths around the dance floor with very well dressed families. One of the sons, from a nearby table asked me to dance. He was very tall, good looking, and very nice. We danced to a couple of songs and he returned me to our table. After he left, the mother looked at me and said, "Do you know who you were dancing with?" I said, "No, who?" The father said, "That was the son of the president of Mexico." He kept eyeing me, but we left soon afterwards. It was fun to talk about though!!

Caemaroom Castle, Wales

I met my parents in **Madeira**, the Portuguese island, over spring break in 1970, and traveled to Tobago after Christmas a few months earlier. One night in Madeira, I don't know what happened to my father and me, we certainly weren't drinking, but we got the giggles. We had had a really fun night with some people we met at the hotel. We were going upstairs in the elevator and my father got this twinkle in his eye. Upon disembarking, we started marching, yes, like in a band, singing "Seventy-Six Trombones in a Big Parade", my mother trailing behind thinking we were ridiculous. We turned around and went back down the hall and mom went in their room. Dad said, "I've always wanted to do this!" In Europe, if you wanted your shoes shined, you simply put them outside your room at night and in the morning, they reappeared, polished to perfection. He looked at the shoes. I eyed them, and said, "Oh, yes, me too". With that, we proceeded to switch all the shoes. There were probably about 10 rooms with shoes outside. We switched all ten rooms, and not with the ones next door. I'm sure the next morning it was mayhem at the front desk. And, we didn't feel a pang of guilt. It was one of my fondest memories of my dad!

The summer of 1970, after my graduation, my parents took me back to Europe; England, Ireland, and Scotland. Once again, we loved England but only spent a little time in London since Ireland and Scotland were our primary destinations this time. On the way to Scotland we passed Queen Elizabeth on her train. Very exciting, although we didn't see a thing of interest. Scotland was dreary and rainy and sort of "drab." But, Ireland was gorgeous. There really is nothing like the Emerald hills of Ireland. I was fascinated by the Gypsy wagons and their Caravans. We traveled across the entire country from west (Shannon) to east (Dublin). We stayed in castles and saw Power's Court, the Ring of Kerry, and I kissed the Blarney Stone. No small feat, by the way, you lay back on a rock on the top of Blarney Castle and they lower you by your feet so you kiss it! Thank God, I had the where with all to wear slacks! We ended in Dublin, and once again were lavishly entertained by the manager of Bank of America. We went to their home which is still today one of my favorite houses I have ever seen. It was a quaint, warm English Tudor with a balcony circling the entire living room area that led to second story rooms and bedrooms.

Kissing the Blarney Stone, Ireland

We were also invited to the US Ambassadors home for a cocktail party. We had always heard that it was difficult for these managers of foreign countries to acclimate back to a US post. You can see why. They were always immediately part of the elite American social circles in foreign countries, and in those days, at least, treated almost like royalty. More travels to come with my father and Jack.

CHAPTER 15
HAWAII

Lucille, Marshal, Charise, 1967

In 1959, we all went to Hawaii, my parents had gone the year before and fell in love with the islands. We stayed in a cottage at the Halekulani Hotel and that started a lifelong love affair. Starting in 1964, my parents and I spent every August in room 30-1 at the Halekulani. It was right off the beach and had two bedrooms and a lanai so it was very spacious and comfortable for the month we were there. I surfed every day for about five hours and then palled around with friends at night. The hotels took turns putting on dances once a week and all the kids went. The same families returned every year, so we all knew each other and some became life-long friends. We had several Hawaiian friends, as well, and attended a traditional Hawaiian wedding complete with the aunt and uncle singing the Hawaiian Wedding Song from a balcony. It was magnificent. We were the only Haoles (white folks, ad they used to say) there. My sisters all came over at one time or another with their husbands and spent a week or two.

A fun memory was sitting out all day on the beach waiting for Julie Andrews to come in on the catamaran between the Halekulani and the Reef Hotel. She was filming "Hawaii" (1966) and I couldn't wait to see her. I was thirteen, and had seen "Mary Poppins" eight times two years before. Unfortunately, my back was to the sun, and I had a lower bikini than I had worn before. I got burned on top of where my skin had already burned and peeled. The result? Second degree burns! I had to wear a sterile bandage for a week around my middle, then Saran Wrap over it for another week, and could not go near the water. For years, I was known as the Saran Wrap Girl. I was even walking my nephew, John Michael Wagner, a few months later in Santa Rosa, CA, and a

Lucille, Charise, Marshal 1965

young girl came up to me and said, "You're the Saran Wrap Girl from Hawaii!" What a claim to fame that was!

The swimming and snorkeling were amazing; the fish had such vibrant colors. I learned to surf and had my own Harbor board with a psychedelic skeg (fin). I still have it. It is a long board, but with very thin side rails, so it is very mobile. Jeff Clark (Maverick's surf Competition founder and world renowned surfer) tells me it is a collector's item now. Harbors were fine boards. One day, I was surfing at "Threes", off the shore from the Reef Hotel, in seven foot waves, the largest I ever surfed. I wiped out and covered my head and crunched bringing my knees up to protect myself from being hit on the head with the board after it shot up in the air. I was in the prescribed position, but the nose of my board hit the water and whipped up between my elbows and knees and got me straight in the nose. I passed out in the water. Luckily my friend, "Grubby" Glen Mitchell, pulled me up by the hair and laid me over his board until I came too. I was more scared of showing my mother my nose than I was of the accident! Fortunately, nothing was broken or mis-shapen, it just really hurt and gave me a couple of black eyes.

Conrad Hilton arranged for me to swim in the lagoon with the dolphins at the newly opened Kahala Hilton Hotel in 1964. It was amazing! But, the dolphins often towed us on our surfboards out to the waves at Wikiki, as well. The waves are about a quarter mile off shore at Waikiki, so it was always a welcome treat to not have to paddle that far. They played with us and jumped over our boards, watching us, and "talking" to us.

We spent three Christmases in Hawaii as well. New Year's in Hawaii is quite fun. The fire crackers go off all day and night until after midnight! My first boyfriend lived on Kalaniiki Street and had a car, so I saw even more of the island. We often went to the north shore to Waimea Bay and Haleiwa. Haleiwa, the home of Shaved Ice!! There was a little store that sold it in a paper cone with all the assorted topping choices. Snow Cones on the mainland never tasted as good as the Hawaiian Shaved

Ice! At Waimea Bay there was the ocean, but also across the road and up a driveway, the water falls. In those days, Weimea Falls were privately owned by a family who let us go up anytime we wanted. The falls included one beautiful 25-foot fall that we could climb up and jump or dive from into a deep pool below. And, down in the bay was also a very large rock from which we would dive. The rock had an underwater cave that included a pass-through from one side to the other. You had to make it in one breath because it was all underwater. You also had to avoid kicking the roof of the cave or you would slice your foot on the corral. The water was so clear you could see the octopuses watching you from the corner of the cave. It was an adrenaline rush for sure to get through safely. The water was so clear in the bay that one day I started to dive for a beer can thinking it was one of those miniature ones they used to put on the straw hats as decoration. After about fifteen feet, I realized it was a regular sized can about forty feet down. I, of course, gave up and turned back to the surface.

My parents and I became members of the Hawaiian Soaring Club and went soaring along the cliffs on the north shore. If you have never gone soaring, do it. It is quite startling to be in a plane with no engine noise. It is silent and you don't realize how accustomed to the noise of the airplane you are, until there is none.

My parents were friends with Northrup and Myrtle Castle, of the original Castle and Cook family. They lived on the big island in Volcano. We visited their plantation many times. They would take us to the volcano, Kilauea, once after it erupted, and we walked along the raised wooden pathways. We visited the beautiful black sand beaches and watched the wild boars in the jungle. We picked strawberries on their farm and swam in their concrete, full sized, above ground pool. It was strange, and we would access it by a wooden staircase. Their house was made of stone and stucco and was always damp in the downstairs guest unit where we stayed. The most memorable meal we shared was a dinner when I was six with the whole family there. My sisters started whispering around the table and it soon got to me. "These are Rocky Mountain oysters!" I said, "What are those?" The response was,

"Bull testicles"! I think we all politely moved them around on our plate. I had already eaten one. I can't say that it was awful or anything, I really don't remember. I just know I only ate one after "getting the word."

The Castle's had a twin-engine airplane and would fly over and pick us up from Oahu. They originally had a single engine, but after going down off the coast of Molokai, they bought a twin engine. Going to Maui for lunch one day Northrup started teaching me to fly. He showed me the altimeter dial after I climbed 500 feet without knowing it. He taught me to bank left and right, and then had me bring it down to 100 feet over the runway before taking over. Then he let me fly all the way back to Honolulu. It was really fun an he said I had a good knack for it. I often thought about taking up flying after that, but never did.

Hawaii has a very special place in my heart. I am glad I was raised there, part time, at the time I was. We had the run of the island and could go anywhere without entrance fees or anyone stopping us. Well, maybe that farmer that we stole the watermelon from on the north shore was not all that thrilled, but it was the best tasting watermelon I have ever had! I returned often, even after I was married and had my children. Byron said his first sentence there the day we heard Elvis Presley died, and Tamara was conceived there. Jack and I took all the kids one Thanksgiving, but it had already started to change. I have not been back since. So many memories of the "old Hawaii."

CHAPTER 16
CHARISE'S ADULT YEARS

I was the juggler in the "Juggler of Notre Dame" the annual Castilleja Christmas pageant my senior year of high school. I want to briefly tell you the story because I have always thought it was so special. During the Middle Ages, each year, the townsfolk of a small village would bring what they hoped was the "perfect

gift" and lay it at the feet of a statue of the Virgin Mary in a chapel. The farmers brought wheat, the merchants brought urns, and the royalty brought jewels and crowns. There was a troupe of jugglers that performed outside the chapel. After everyone leaves the chapel, one little juggler stays behind. He proceeds to dance his heart out for the Virgin Mary, literally, and takes his last breath at the foot of the statue. The towns people hear the church bells ringing, and come rushing back into the church. At the stroke of midnight, the Virgin Mary comes to life and

Beth Livermore, Madonna, Charise, The Juggler, 1969 in the Juggler of Notre Dame

blesses the "perfect gift." The girl that plays the Madonna stands perfectly still for 45 minutes, you forget she isn't really

a statue, and when she moves, and bows, and lowers her hands over the juggler, then raises them to heaven, lifting up his soul, it is truly a magical moment. I wish I could see it again.

I also, had the lead in the spring school play, "Take Her, She's Mine." I was on the Spirit Team, played volleyball, softball, basketball, and competed in swimming. I was very good at synchronized swimming (I can still do it today) and took fencing.

The summer of my senior year, I was a debutante at both the San Francisco Presbyterian Ball and then the Peninsula Ball in Los Altos. This was not really something I was interested in, but my parents wanted it. Having said that, it is how I met **Henri Louis "Bud" Werner (4/16/1951-)** And, the parties were spectacular. One debutante's parents rented the Playland at the Beach Fun House for the night, and another's father owned Marine World. We got free run of the place one night with shows, dancing, and all the food concessions were open just for us.

Charise and Bud, 1970, Peninsula Ball

Charise, Bud, Marsha, Jack, Valerie, Dobie, Loralyn, Johnny, 1973

I proceeded to the University of the Pacific that fall, but transferred in the spring to College of Notre Dame. I graduated from CND, Cum Laude in History, after spending my junior year at University of California at Davis. I wanted to be near my fiancé, Bud. We were married August 18, 1973, right before my senior year

Charise and Marshal III

of college.

Werner Genealogy

Bud's great grandparents on his father's side were **Henry Rosentahl (1874-1934) and Amelia Meyer Rosenthal (1864-1938) and Samuel Werner (1867-?) and Helen Koholenherner Werner (1869-?)**. Grandparents were **Jack Werner (1898-1973),** known as the father of Periodontistry at College of Physicians and surgeons in San Francisco, and **Myrell Rosenthal Werner (1902-1987)**. Their son was Bud's father, **Jack Werner 5/13/1923-3/23/2006**), a well-known dentist at 450 Sutter in San Francisco.

Weyl Genealogy

Louis Levin (1828-1889) was married to **Frederika Newfield Levin (1828-1909).** They were Bud's great great grandparents. Their daughter was Esther Levin Weyl. Great grandparents were **Bernardo Weyl (1860-1945) and Esther Levin Weyl (1862-1949)**. And Israel Friedman and Esther Leah Morris Friedman. Grandparents were **Henri Hellman Weyl (1896-1943),** who owned Sellers Brothers Hardware in San Francisco, and **Blanche Friedman Weyl (1897-1973)**. Their daughter, Bud's mother, is **Jacqueline Lou Weyl Werner (6/23/1924-)**.

Bud's parents were **Jack Werner 5/13/1923-3/23/2006)** and **Jacqueline Lou Weyl Werner (6/23/1924-)**. I absolutely loved my in laws. My father-in-law and I hit it off from the get go. We had a very special bond, that is hard to describe. I admired and loved him so much and miss him to this day. A kinder more loving father, I have never known, I also love my now ex mother-in-law, Jackie. She was born with not a bad bone in her body. Jackie had a large family with many aunties. They were all huggers and kissers. You

Jacqueline Lou Weyl Werner (6/23/1924-) and Jack Werner 5/13/1923-3/23/2006

never entered a room without going around and kissing and hugging everyone. This was something we didn't do in my family. My mother was Irish and affectionate, but my father came from a very stuffy upbringing. The Werner's taught me to be outwardly affectionate and then I started doing it with my own family. My sisters didn't know quite what to make of it at first, nor my father. But, they adjusted none the less, and I think it brought all of us closer together. I thank the Werner's for that exposure.

We had **Byron Hale Werner on November 30, 1975** and **Tamara Werner on May 8, 1978**. Bud was my best friend, but I wanted more passion out of a marriage, and we were separated in September of 1981 and then divorced. I am happy to say we have always remained friends and put our children first. When people ask "why"? My answer has always been; that is the easiest question to ask and the hardest to answer. I would be remiss here if I didn't state that he is a wonderful, nurturing, father and grandfather. My children and grandchildren are lucky to have him in their lives. They are also lucky to have Lynn Kaplan Werner (9/8/60-), Bud's present wife, in their lives. They have two twin boys, Zachary and Charlie born 11/18/2000.

Byron Hale Werner (1975-) and Tamara Werner (1978-)

It is not my place to tell the life stories of those living, but since I am their mother, I want to tell two stories about my children.

Byron knew what he wanted to do by the age of eight. Tamara used to say, "Well, not everyone knows what they wanted to be since they were a sperm, Mom!" Both my children were blessed with a sharp wit and wicked sense of humor. And, she was right, he was involved in film from then on, and I've never been more proud than when I hear his colleagues talk about his talent and how he achieves the scene he wants through polite and succinct requests.

But, here is my funny Byron story. When he was fifteen, we were up at Tahoe at our A-Frame house and Jack and I went into town while the kids were at the rec center in Northstar. I had a couple of Margaritas, and they did not hit me well. I don't ever remember getting that drunk and that sick. I don't know if it was the altitude or the Triple sec they put in the Margarita, or an empty stomach, but Jack had to pull off the road for me on the way home. My children had never even seen me tipsy, let alone smashed. I walked into the house, Byron wanted to tell me something, and I quickly said, "Wait a minute, I will be right back." Our bedroom was downstairs from the main floor and I quickly started to run down the stairs. I got as far as the first landing and vomited again. Byron reeled around and said, "Oh gross," or something like that. The following Monday as I was driving the kids to school, Byron made a long list of things he needed me to do for him that day. I said, "Jeez, what are you going to do for me when I get all this done?" He immediately quipped, "Keep quiet about Saturday night, Mom!" I said, "Ok, good point." It was pretty funny and shows you his sense of humor.

Although Tamara has a great sense of humor and can toss out barbs with the best of the boys, as seen above about her brother knowing what he wanted to do in life, my Tamara story, is not funny, on the contrary. When she was just three years old, my mother died of cancer. My parents had been traveling in Europe and after returning she died less than thirty-six hours later, on a Saturday. On Monday, I went out to get the mail and there was a postcard from her. I started crying and dropped to my knees on my living room floor. I was sobbing full force by the time Tamara came out of her bedroom and reached the top of the stairs above me. I still remember Tamara in her navy dress with red smocking, her long hair in pigtails, hand on the railing, starting to descend the stairs above me. She calmly said, "What's wrong, Mommy?" The hysterical crying would have scared the life out of most three year olds. She walked down the stairs speaking very slowly to me. I said while sobbing, "I g-g-got a p-p-postcard f-f-from-m-m-my m-m-mo-t-t-t-ther!" She walked up to me, and put her arms around me, rubbing my back with one hand and holding my head to her chest with the other. She very calmly said, "That's okay, Mommy, you cry. I'm here." I still get tears in my eyes and a lump in my throat every time I tell this story. She was only three years old. Years later when she got her masters in counseling I felt like the circle had been completed. There was never a person more suited.

Byron, a cinematographer, is married to a wonderful woman, and one I also consider my good friend, **Amy Muckinhaupt Werner (November 15, 1975-)**. They have two children; **Annabelle Grace Werner (January 23, 2010-)** and **Sadie Rose Werner (May 30, 2012-)**.

Tamara is a counselor specializing in women and men with eating disorders. She was married to **Adam Christopher Duarte (10/21/1982-)**, they divorced in 2018. They Have two children: **Jacob Hale Duarte (11/30/2005-)** and **Chloe Jane Duarte (2/14/2007-)**

✳✳✳

While Bud and I were married, I went to work for a man that would be a big influence on me, and is still my best male friend today, he just turned 90! I have always loved animals, and went to work for a veterinarian after graduating college. I did everything from receptionist to surgical assistant and loved it. I still worked for John Weinmann, DMV after the kids were born on Saturdays and then a few days a week when the kids went to school. There are a few cute stories that most will enjoy.

The first, A little girl came into the hospital and put her kitten up on the counter. The receptionist said, "Well hello there, what is your name, and what is your kitten's name?" the little girl said, "My name is Mary, and his name is Hemorrhoid, because my mommy says he's a pain in the butt!"

My favorite Dr. Weinmann story occurred when I was eight and a half months pregnant with Byron. Ralph Thompson came in with his St. Bernard ho was old and not in good shape. The doctor determined the best thing for the animal was to euthanize him; he was just too far gone. Ralph said his good-byes, paid the fee and left. We walked his dog into the back where the freezer was, an upright freezer. The pet memorial people picked up whatever deceased animals every Thursday. This was a Tuesday. We knew this was a problem, but couldn't bring ourselves to have Ralph wait for two days after making this difficult decision. We gently had the dog lay on the floor, he was too big to get up onto a table and he would have hated it, so while I petted him, Dr. Weinmann euthanized him. He was also too big to fit into a black 40-gallon garbage bag, as would be standard practice. The decision was made to put him in the freezer with no bag. So, I removed the one animal, a cat, from the freezer, and my ice cream. (I was 8 months pregnant, I needed my ice cream fix.) I removed all the freezer shelves, and John and I managed to get the dog into the freezer sitting upright. We closed the door, let out an exhausted breath and walked away. The freezer door flew open, and out came the dog hitting us in the back of the knees, and we both fell forward, him catching me before I hit the ground with my rather large stomach! We started all over, only this time when we had him inside, I laid on the floor on my back, with my enormous stomach sticking out, my feet on the door, keeping it closed, while John tied a rope around the freezer to secure it. He helped me up, I was exhausted, but as I turned around, I realized the cat was still sitting on a shelf, outside the freezer. I always thought this would have made a great "Saturday Night Live" skit. And, yes, we did it all over again wedging the cat behind the dog's shoulder blades. Thank God it wasn't a chest freezer, we never would have gotten the dog out!

John M. Weinmann
(1927-)

***

Charise and Connie, 1972

Connie and Charise

I spent quite a bit of time with Conrad Hilton in his later years when I was in my teens and early twenties. He visited us, we visited him, and we spent time with him in Hawaii as well. He arranged so I could swim with the dolphins at the Kahala Hilton, as previously mentioned. He would always take us to dinner, he especially liked the Bimbos 365 Club in San Francisco. In all the years he took us to dinner, I NEVER once saw him presented with a check! All the restauranteurs where honored that he chose their restaurant in which to dine. As I sat at his breakfast table (a table for 12), his dining room table sat 24, I had to drink all my milk before I could be excused. This was when I was 18. I spent a weekend with him at his house with my fiancé, Bud Werner. We were in separate but adjoining suites. Gorgeous rooms. He was the sweetest man and seemed so naïve. Obviously, there was another business side to Conrad Hilton that I never only occasionally saw.

Conrad Hilton

When we traveled, as we did a lot since I was born a month before my father's 50th birthday, and he retired when he was 54, my parents would stay in hotels that represented the countries, but once per trip we would stay in a Hilton. We took bets as to whether the portrait of Connie in the lobby would have him with or without his toupee. And, my father would send him a list of repairs. "The shower head in Room such and such at the Berlin Hilton needs cleaning. I cleaned it with a bobby pin and now it is better!" I remember once Dad got an English muffin. My father said, "It is one English muffin, Connie, the menu called it two English muffins, it has two halves by definition!" They laughed about that one and Connie had the menu description

**Lucille, Connie, his friend Sally
1970, Presbyterian Ball**

changed. Seeing as how we would be traveling for several weeks, and with a child, my mother would do laundry at night in the bathtub. She complained that there was nowhere to hang her stockings and our under things accept on the shower rod and then they would drip onto the floor of the bathroom. Connie had someone invent that little clothes line that sits in that round chrome holder and you can pull across the center of the tub lengthwise so you can hang your laundry and preserve the bathroom floor. You can all thank my mother for that one!

Connie wrote me letters often and he once gave me a small book entitled "Para Ti". It was in Spanish and he translated every line to English by hand. Can you imagine? Like he didn't have anything else to do! He gave the most magnificent clocks to my sister and me for our weddings. They were both gold mantle clocks and we both still have them. The newspaper picture, at the beginning of this section, was taken when I was a debutante, in June 1970, at the Presbyterian Ball at the Sheraton Palace in San Francisco. He, also, came to my wedding and we danced and had a wonderful time. I have so many fond memories of him. He was a kind, generous, interesting man, and always interested in your life.

※※※

At this point, I want to tell you about another person who has always had a great influence on my life, my best friend. Susan Janette Foster (9/1/1949-). We met when I was three and she was six. We are still best friends today, 64 years later. Her family, also has an interesting history.

Susie, I am the only one allowed to call her that, lived below us on Tiptoe Lane. Her father, Lee Foster, worked for Bethlehem Steel and her mother, Dora Fabian Foster, was the first female butcher at Debuque's in South San Francisco. They met while Lee was serving in the US Army as a mechanic under General Patton during World War II. Dora came from a well to do family in Germany. They had a home in Berlin and a farm in the country. Hitler's soldiers often partied at their house in Berlin, and Dora would throw roses on Hitler from their balcony when he paraded through the streets. They thought Hitler would save Germany. He had not started persecuting the Jews at this time. Once he started, and Jews had to where sashes identifying themselves, then the Fabians saw Hitler's true colors. Susie's grandfather started smuggling Jews in a false bottom wagon to a location where they could escape Germany. Susan's uncle, Hans, served in the German army. He was captured early on in the war, and in typical Hanes fashion, spent the rest of the war in England assigned to watch over a general's horses. Most likely there was beer or libations of some kind to be found. Never a more affable man would I know!

Charise and Susie, 2018 Wearing our half hearts that Susie bought us around 1998

Because the family was influential with the military, Dora's sister, Inga's husband was a pilot in the German Luftwaffe, a truck was sent to pick them up and get them out of Germany. The Russians were coming and torching all the towns they went through. Dora was told they were leaving and going to climb over the Alps to Switzerland. Being sixteen, Dora could not decide which clothes to take and proceeded to put on layer after layer. She was the only one warm throughout their journey. But, it was back in Berlin after the war ended, while volunteering for the American Stars and Stripes, that Dora met Lee. She came home to California with him and settled in South San Francisco, and later her widowed sister, Inga, followed. Then Hans and their mother came over. Dora's father never made it to the U.S.

This was my second family. Susie has two brothers; Peter Lee Foster (10/1/1954-) and Nikki Johann Foster (12/30/1957-). We were thick as thieves, playing almost daily. We had a Dare Devil's Club and would dare each other to do things that now make me cringe. Like walking across rocky creeks 20 feet in the air on a water pipe! We dressed alike and went everywhere together. We never cared if one of us paid for the popcorn at the movies, because the next time the other would.

We had a maid, Mae Filipe, who loved wrestling. She would take Susie and me to the Cow Palace to see matches. Our favorites were Hay Stack Calhoun and Ray Stevens. We were quite the wrestling connoisseurs. When Susie was in high school, she got mad at her mother and lived in my room for a week without my parents knowing. She did a lot of hiding in the shower. I would help her with her English homework and she would help me with my Math. We learned to ski together and would leave at 3am in the morning and drive to South Shore Lake Tahoe to get to Heavenly when the lifts opened. She spoke fluent German so that came in handy listening to the ski instructors talk about asking us for dates when they didn't think we knew what they were talking about. She would answer them in German before they actually asked, causing great laughter between us.

Her father kept building them new houses, that I had to help with if I wanted to play with her. He built two, close by, and then bought the coolest house of all. An English Tudor with a real slate roof built by Col. Cotton that had a real cave off the living room. And, I mean a real cave that went to the top of the mountain! We used to play in this cave all the time as children, when we got up enough courage to ask Col. Cotton if we could come in. We were sort of scared of him, but drummed up the nerve every few months to ring his door bell. Then, when we were in high school

Lee bought the house and property., which was also very close to my house. I went on day trips with the Fosters, Susie came to the Ranch every summer and after we stopped going to the Ranch, I went with the Fosters for a couple of weeks to our Ranch! Susie was part of our family, and I hers. My mother adored her, all my sisters know her well, she is like another sister.

Susie and I have remained close all these years. We were each other's Maid/Matron of Honor in our weddings, she is my children's God Mother, and I would call her mother almost weekly when she got older. Her parents moved to Utah and her father passed away at 93 on June 6, 2017. A side note on her father. He called me Therese my whole life. Never once did he call me Charise. We would all correct him and he would say, "Oh yes." And the next time he saw me he would call me Therese?? Her mother passed away at 93 on January 16, 2018. For my birthday,

"Para Ti", personally translated for me by Conrad Hilton

shortly before her mother passed away she gave me a sapphire and diamond ring that belonged to her mother. I told her "You can't do this!" She said, "The hell I can't, my mother thought of you as her other daughter. We all have September birthdays, she would want you to have this." The story doesn't end there. My next birthday when at my house for my retirement party with all my children there, she proceeds to gift me a diamond bracelet and earrings. I say, "Susie, no way!" "She says, "read the card." In her card, she explains that she doesn't like jewelry, she never wears it, which is true, she then says, you love jewelry, you wear it, you enjoy it. My mother would love to have her jewelry worn by someone who loves it and loved her. You have granddaughters. My mother only has one, and she will inherit plenty of her jewelry. She said, I don't have any children, but you have three granddaughters that she and her jewelry can live on through. Of course, at this point, we were all crying. So, Chloe, Annabelle, and Sadie, this is for you, so you know where that jewelry came from and a little history of its owner and giver, your mommy and daddy's Godmother.

✳ ✳ ✳

I joined Peninsula Children's Theatre in 1980, the first PCTA brat to join. I was in it for a year before my mother died, so she got to see me in my first PCTA play.

Skip Bogart, Charise 1989 my year as president

Even though I was the youngest, by far, I never played the ingénue because I couldn't sing. I had more fun. I played Piglet, Cinderella's cat, Snow White's rabbit, and the Hen that laid the golden egg. All the children wanted to meet the animal in the lobby after the play and get my autograph. It was really cute. The group was disbanded around 2000, but for the last years, I have put together a luncheon. Once or twice a year all the ladies gather at a restaurant so we can see each other. I have never known such a supportive and close knit group.

✱✱✱

I have two other best friends that have been a big part of my life as well. We have been friends for over 35 years. Lorrie Whitenight and Penny Wright Mulligan. We met when our husbands or boyfriends were colleagues in a financial firm in San Francisco. We went out with our group, had lunches, and went to parties together. Penny was 10 years younger than Lorrie and me and one night we all went to the ladies room together in a club on Knob Hill. Penny exclaimed, "We'll always be friends!" Lorrie and I looked in the mirror at one another and said, "Penny, our men are in business together, if something happens to their relationship, ours will fall by the wayside. Theirs is the primary relationship." Well, sure enough their business relationship changed, but boy were Lorrie and I wrong! Because over 35 years later, we are still best friends and celebrate every birthday with a lunch. We take a picture each time and the birthday girl is in the middle. Lorrie and I are Godmothers to Penny's oldest daughter, Taylor and sort of unofficial ones to Haley. So, another life lesson, when you find true friends that are with you through thick and thin, always there to support you, you make sure you keep them. You make sure you stay in contact and see each other as often as possible. Friends like these are hard to come by. I am very lucky to have a few other close friends, male and female that are very precious to me. If they are reading this book, they will know who they are.

Lorrie, Charise, Penny, 2019

✱✱✱

My personalized license plate was and still is EXUBRNT. It probably best describes my personality. As previously mentioned, I was nicknamed Princess Leather Foot, Waf-n-Pay, Parnelli (okay, so I have a lead foot), and Sunshine. But, always called Charise. I hated Sherry, or Therese. Why, when you are given a beautiful name would you want to change it? That is not conceited because I didn't name myself. My mother and my sisters did. In the baby name book it had Charis, pronounced "Haris", the Greek Goddess of Grace. My mother said why not put an "e" on the end and pronounce the "c". My sisters yelled Yeah, and that was how I was named.

✳✳✳

I met Jack on March 9, 1982. A friend set us up, and we met for a cocktail at The Customs House Restaurant in Foster City where I was a Banquet Director. We had a great time, but it wasn't until I walked him to his car in the parking lot that I began to get an inkling of what the future might bring. I am a little bit country and a little bit city. I am equally at home at a black-tie affair as I am on a horse in the country. This is not that uncommon for women, but I maintain, it is for men. Men are either one or the other. Bud was a city boy, I loved the Ranch, he did not. A constant bone of contention during our marriage. Back to the parking lot. Jack, in his three-piece suit and tie, walked up to his 1981 Renegade CJ7 Jeep and put on a baseball cap. I thought, Really? When I went home, I called my best friend, Susie, and told her about it!

After working for The Custom's House, the manager, Lynn Merrit, and I founded a company called Promotions with Pizzazz. We had a great office in the city and worked as consultants for restaurants, a jewelry company, the San Francisco Warriors, Giants, and Forty-Niners, as well as the Oakland Invaders. We had a fabulous cardboard picnic box colored as a cable car filled with Gallo salami, Sonoma Jack cheese, Parisianne sour dough bread, Mendocino Honey mustard,

Charise and Lynn on the cover of a Restaurant magazine

Ghirardelli chocolate and red and white Robert Mondavi wine. We had two booths at the Stanford hosted Super Bowl XIX. But, it wasn't bringing in enough money to support a family, so in 1986 we dissolved the partnership. Lynn was another big influence on my life, and I must say, we had a blast while working together. He went on to be the head of sports marketing for Nike, and is known as the "most powerful man in basketball". I am very proud of his accomplishments. It is a lifelong friendship that I cherish.

I then went back to work for Dr. Weinmann and the pet hospital to get it ready for sale, and then stayed on with the new vet, Dr. Craig Machado, for a few years. It was perfect while the kids were in school, because I worked Monday, Tuesday, and Thursday unless I had something better to do with my kids.

I tried retiring but was bored stiff and driving Jack crazy. I applied for the CEO of the Half Moon Bay Coastside Chamber of Commerce and after six weeks and forty-three applicants was offered the job. I wish for everyone to have a job that is perfect for them. That is what the Chamber was, and I am proud of my accomplishments over the almost twenty-three years. We became a visitors' bureau as well. I founded a Hotel Business Improvement District, established a foundation 501c3, created a dynamic Education Committee with everyone at the table, started the Coastside Emergency Action Program for disaster preparedness (now used as a model), expanded bussing on the Coast, cut red tape for businesses with the city, county, and state, started several new events, Life Skills at the high schools, and planted the Highway One medians (a 15 year project). I served on the Western Association of Chamber Executives board for six years and on their foundation for eight. WACE awarded me the William Hammond Award, only given to one executive a year in the western fifteen states. At retirement, I was read into the U. S. Congressional records by Rep. Jackie Speier as well as accommodations from the California State Assembly, Senate, San Mateo County Board of Supervisors, and the Half Moon Bay City Council. I also received the Mayor's Award and a special award from the Boys & Girls' Club. After I announced my retirement, a councilman told my replacement that it would not be easy for her to fill my shoes, but probably easier for them because, "Everyone knew that going against Charise McHugh was political suicide." That statement made me very happy, I did my job well!

Life Advice from Charise

To my children, grandchildren, great grandchildren, and beyond if you are reading this. First advice is: You have a choice every morning when you wake up. You can be a victim, have a bad attitude, think in the terms of "Oh, poor me", and the world is against me. OR, you can wake up determined to make it a good day, think positive, have a good attitude, be the best you can possibly be, and make a difference to your fellow man. The latter will make you a happier, more productive, and a more loved person than the former. And, you will feel good about yourself. Remember, giving to others really is the best reward. The sooner you realize that it is not all about you, the happier you will be. I cannot emphasize this enough. I used to hear "Giving is better than receiving", and I thought, okay, I understand, but I love getting presents. And, I still do. I just think I now get greater pleasure seeing my children's and grandchildren's faces when I give them something they really wanted, or that I was creative about finding. I smile when I find it, I smile when I buy it, I smile when I wrap it, and I smile when they open it. Giving to those less fortunate is the best reward of all. Serve on that board, work in that soup kitchen, donate to that cause.

Second piece of advice: Don't procrastinate. Just do it and get it done. It will take less time if you do it right away rather than waiting until the last minute. And, you have time to make it better or correct it if need be. When I was in the Chamber business I had a saying, that was usually spoken quietly to myself. "Your procrastination does not make my emergency."

And, third advice topic: Say you're sorry. That is not an admission of guilt. Sometimes you had nothing to do with it, but you are sorry it happened to the other person. And, if you made a mistake, say so. People respect that. It is not a sign of weakness, it is a sign of strength. People spend way too much time on blaming someone else. We all make mistakes, say so and move on. That takes a stronger person with a confident ego. Be that person.

Think about it, these may not make sense to you if you read this when you are really young, but one day it will. And, when it does, look upwards so I can see your knowing, smiling face.

CHAPTER 17
JACK

John Dillon McHugh II
(1945-

John D. McHugh II (Jack) was born on December 9, 1945 and grew up in Orange, CT, just outside of New Haven. Jack's father was an attorney and served in the House of Representatives for the State of Connecticut. Jack remembers his father drawing up wills at the kitchen table at night for friends, and received in payment a couple dozen eggs or whatever the client could afford. I have always told Jack that he was raised in the "Leave It to Beaver" house (old television show of the perfect family) with soccer dad and apple pie baking mom. He truly had a wonderful childhood absent of the drama with which I grew up.

McHugh History

Jack's great great grandfather Bernard Reilly (9/23/1823-3/22/1886), made his living in real estate in New Haven, Connecticut. He married Margaret Martin, born in Ireland, birth date unknown, but death date was 1/8/1898. They are buried in St. Bernard's Cemetery, West Haven, CT. Speaking of the cemetery, one good family story, was that Bernard went to the town council and asked permission to build a cemetery. One of the Councilmen said, "But, I thought you said you were buying up all this land for friends!" Mr. Reilly answered, "I did. You never asked me if they were alive or dead!" Jack's great grandfather was Peter McHugh, birthdate unknown, but he died 1/13/1888. In 1864, he was the first Irish Catholic alderman for the City of New Haven.

John Dillon McHugh
(1903-1974)

The family was originally from county Leitrim in Ireland. And, his grandfather, John F. McHugh (dates unknown) was the town clerk of New Haven. John married Margaret Dillon, daughter of Michael Dillon, who owned a shoe store in New Haven. They had one son, Jack's father, John Dillon McHugh (1/6/1903-6/14/1974), an attorney in New Haven. John married Lorraine Cashman (6/1/1918-1/22/1997) in 1937.

Cashman History

Jack's great great great grandparents were Patrick (Patt) Cashman (b.1810) and Ellen (Nelly) Green Cashman (b.1810) both of Fermoy Parish, Chapel Hill, Ireland. They married on February 12, 1832. No birth and death dates are known for them. His other great great great grandparents were Maurice and Ellen Ford Walsh. There are conflicting records, also showing a James (1814-????) and Mary Dalsey (Daly) Walsh. Since a family member deemed there was more evidence that it was Maurice and Ellen, I am using their names and information. This was researched by Lorraine's second cousin, Germaine "Gerry" M. Grady; their grandfathers were brothers. Maurice was born in 1814 and Ellen in 1815, both of Fermoy (possibly Fermay) Parrish, Barrack Hill. They were married in County Cork in 1834 and probably died in the Potato Famine between 1847 and 1851 in County Cork, Ireland. Patt and Nelly had Maurice Peter Cashman (9/1835-2/14/1902). Maurice was born in Fermoy Parish, County Cork, Ireland and came to America in the mid 1850's. He became a US citizen on March 7, 1867 at 31 years of age. He married Hannah Walsh (1837-2/8/1895) on October 9, 1862 at St. John's Church. Hannah probably emigrated with her cousins to New Haven in early 1862. Maurice was a laborer and was then involved in real estate in Hamden, CT. He set up a grocery and meat market for his son James Cashman. Another son, Thomas Cashman, worked as a blacksmith. Their third son, Edward J. Cashman

Lorraine Cashman McHugh (1918-1997)

(6/11/1868-2/2/1907) married Catherine C. Burke in 1894. They had a son named Lawrence S. Cashman (7/20/1895-12/21/1935) who married Rita Adams Cashman in 1913. Lawrence Cashmen was a firefighter in New Haven. Jack's great grandmother on his grandmother Rita's side was Elizabeth O'Sullivan Adams, who, also, resided in New Haven. Lawrence and Rita gave birth to Lorraine Cashman (6/1/1918-1/22/1997), and her brother, Edward "Brud" was born in 1919, he died October 30, 1979. "Brud" was never married and was a Hamden, CT policeman with badge #1.

Jack, after high school, took a trip to California before starting college, and his mother called to tell him his uncle wanted him. Jack said, "Uncle Fred?", and his mother said, "No, Uncle Sam." Jack served two years in the Army and figured if he was going to Vietnam, he should be the best trained soldier possible. He went to Light Weapons Infantry Training and Jump School to become a paratrooper. Then he was shipped to Panama for Jungle Warfare Training. He was in the 508th Battalion, a division of the 82nd Airborne.

One story that I love was when he was in Panama training for Vietnam, they were doing a parachute jump out of a C-130. There is no rank when you are in line for a jump. The reason is if someone freezes in the doorway, then the last man out may jump into the ocean or enemy territory. So, there was a captain in front of Jack in line to jump and he froze in the doorway. Jack did exactly as trained and put his foot on the guy's ass and pushed hard enough to shove him out of the plane. Even though it was what he was taught and trained to do, he ended up on KP duty peeling potatoes for a month! He learned jungle warfare in Panama and had to survive in the jungle with a gun and a knife. Biting off a chicken's head to drink the blood was one of the more disgusting stories he would regal the kids with at bedtime.

He never went to Vietnam, thank God, because only a few men from his unit came back walking and talking. He picked up a baseball bat for the U.S. Army

Southern Command and the Colonel kept pulling his orders because he wanting to keep beating the Navy!

After the Army, he attended American International College, was the co-captain of the football team and a baseball star. A funny story happened one night as Jack and some of his football teammates were at the McHugh house for Lorraine's famous T-Bone steaks. After dinner, they settled in the living room, three of them on the sofa. They chatted with "Mom-bo" (Jack's mother) and then all left. A few minutes later two of them came back and started searching the sofa. Finding nothing, they left and had to report to the other boys that the marijuana joint one of them had in his pocket must have fallen out, and now they couldn't find it. Jack said, "Are you crazy? We have to find it. That's my parent's house!" They looked a second time. Then they had to give up. Jack didn't know the whole story until Mom-bo told it to me about thirteen years later, sitting in our dining room in Half Moon Bay. Here's what happened. Mom-bo found the joint and put it in her apron pocket (1971). She didn't know what to do with it. Her husband was the Chair of the Drug Task Force Committee in the Assembly for the State of Connecticut! How could she dump it? What if someone found it? She kept it in her apron pocket until John McHugh , Jack's father, passed away in 1974! Jack graduated with a business degree in 1972 and a graduate degree in 1973 from AIC.

***

Marcie and Jack, 1972

Jack married his college sweetheart, Marcie, and they moved to California. Marcie Stern McHugh (10/28/50- became a teacher and Jack a financial advisor. They had Joshua Stern McHugh on July 15, 1977. The first thing I think about Josh as a child is cuddling. He was the best cuddler and would just mold to you. Josh followed his dream of raw/organic food and became a chef and then founded his own company. He met Geri Logan in 2012 at a music festival in the Sierras. We are gifted with another great addition to our family. Jaden McHugh was born on 4/8/2014 and Asha Dillon McHugh on 11/16/2015. My favorite Josh story is when Josh was 11 my father passed away. The next morning we were all sitting in our family room and Josh said, "Pops just wasn't having fun anymore." Truer words were never spoken.

Stern History for Joshua Stern McHugh and Descendants Marcie Sheila Stern (McHugh) Plummer was born on October 28, 1950 in Plymouth, MA, the youngest of three. When she was three, the family moved to Winthrop, MA, home of Governor John Winthrop of the Massachusetts Bay Colonies. Marcie attended and graduated from Winthrop High School before attending American International College, where she graduated in 1972 with a BA in English Literature and in 1974 with a Master's Degree in Education. Marcie taught English at Windsor Locks Middle School in Windsor Locks, CT, moving to San Francisco in 1975 with then husband, John McHugh. Their son Joshua Stern McHugh was born July 15, 1977. Marcie taught English at Diablo Valley College and San Ramon Valley High School before becoming an administrator in the Castro Valley Unified School District and Hayward Unified School District. Marcie married Louis Freeman Plummer (11/4/1947-) on September 25, 1982. They had two daughters, Joshua's half-sisters; Jessica Price Plummer (6/4/1983) and Denelle Plummer Shemesh (3/20/1986). Denelle married Yacov Emil Shemesh

Jack, Marcie, Josh 1977

(10/20/1986). Marcie's last seven years in education were spent as Principal of Monterey High School before earning her doctorate in Organizational Leadership with a focus on social justice at Brandman University. Marcie then became a staff member of the Principal Leadership Institute at The University of California at Berkeley.

Stern Genealogy

Marcie's paternal grandparents were Issac and Francis (Fannie) Briteman Stern. Francis and Issac Stern came from a village called Kumminance Podolsk in Belarus, Russia. The village is 20 miles from Kiev. Roasalie, Marcie's mother, always said you did not want to get sick because there was only a horse doctor, and you did not want to walk the 20 miles to Kiev. Issac and Fannie came to America in the early 1900's. They settled in Roxbury, Massachusetts, and later in Boston. Issac was a carpenter. Years later, he worked for Max Adelman. They are listed on the wall at Ellis Island.

Adelman Genealogy

Marcie's maternal grandparents were Sarah Berson Adelman (d. 2/25/1987) and Max Adelm Adelman (d. 4/1972). Marcie's mother is Rosalie Adelman Stern. Sarah was born and emigrated from Vilnius, Lithuania in the early 1900's. Max was born in Grodno, Poland which became part of Russia during his childhood. He emigrated in the early 1900's as well. They settled in Boston, Mass. Max was a contractor, building homes throughout the Boston area. He learned his craft from working as a carpenter for Joseph Kennedy. Rosalie Stern was born August 15, 1923, the youngest of 6. They, too, came through Ellis Island.

Jacob Stern (12/25/19176/1999-) and Rosalie Adelman Stern (8/15/1923), 1945

Jacob and Rosalie were married on September 25, 1945. They were married at the Boston Courthouse. Jacob (Jack) had already joined the Navy and shipped out shortly thereafter. When Jack returned, they lived in Virginia Beach, had two children before his discharge from the Navy. The Stern's settle in Plymouth, MA where Marcie was born. Three years later, they relocated with family close in Winthrop, MA where they lived until 1975, when they retired to West Palm Beach, FL. Jack Stern passed away in June,

1999. Rosalie is 96 years young and resides in West Palm Beach, FL at the writing of this book.

Jack and Marcie divorced in 1980, and he met me on March 9, 1982. Again, Marcie and Jack have remained friends, and Marcie would be one of my first choices as an advocate, if I ever needed one. I truly love the woman and consider her a friend.

✳ ✳ ✳

Jack's siblings are Lawrence Dillon McHugh (9/23/1939-), Judith Ann McHugh Fitzgerald (4/7/1942-), and Peter Michael McHugh (2/14/1949-).

Larry's children are: Lawrence Dillon McHugh (11/30/1964-), no children. Sean Michael McHugh (9/14/1967-), has a daughter Riley Lynn McHugh (11/7/2003-) Michael Patrick McHugh (4/19/1970-), no children

Larry, Lorraine, Judy, Peter, Jack, 1989

Judy's children are: Christopher John Fitzgerald (9/29/1968-), his children are John David Fitzgerald (2/2/2004-) and Meghan Ann Fitzgerald (7/18/2005-). Kevin McHugh Fitzgerald (7/23/1972-) has two sons, Ryan Fitzgerald (9/20/2007-) and Dillon Fitzgerald (8/27/2012-) Timothy Peter Fitzgerald (4/28/1977-) has one son, Jack Fitzgerald (8/27/2012-)

I never knew Jack's father, I wish I had. When I met his mother and siblings, I fell in love with all the McHugh's and FitzGerald's. They accepted me and my children as though we had always been a part of the family. My children were even listed as surviving grandchildren in Mom-bo's obituary, and Byron was a pall bearer right along with Josh and his cousins. Larry, Sr. and I share a birthday, and he has been the CEO for the Middlesex County Chamber of Commerce for the last thirty years. How's that for coincidence? He was also the football coach for Xavier High School and held the record for the most wins of any previous high school coach in the nation. He is an exemplary Chamber executive and a man I greatly admire. The only difference between us in the Chamber world is he was asked to run for governor and has a building the size of a square block named after him at the University of Connecticut and the Chamber building in Middlesex County. His wife is Patty and she is awesome. I am so lucky to have such wonderful in law sisters and brothers. Judy is married to Fitzie (Donald FitzGerald) who is one of the funniest people I know. Always ready with the joke, always with a beer in hand, he is the quintessential Irishman! Judy and I became sisters the first night we met. Never was there a kinder person to walk this earth. And, Peter, is probably one of the most brilliant people I have met. Much like my brother-in-law, Dobie, this is the guy you want to have on your call list if you are ever a contestant on "I Want to Be a Millionaire".

Judy, Tamara, Mom-bo (Lorraine McHugh), Charise, c. 1986

Charise and Jack, 1993

I regret that Jack didn't know my mother, and I never met his father. I feel like I knew Dad-mo from all the stories. And a great Life Skills lesson from Jack's father that I love is: It's one thing to know your strengths, but knowing your weaknesses are far more important. Also, right time, right place. We always told our children, if you don't get out there, you can never be in the right place at the right time. It isn't going to happen with you sitting on the couch!

Obviously, Jack listened to his father. He started out in insurance and moved into Financial Advising. He has had a wonderful career and been extremely successful. I think he has done a magnificent job at balancing his career with his family life. I admire his honesty with his clients. He will never buy or sell a client's assets unless it is the right thing for their portfolio. Most of his clients have become great friends, a testament to the trust they have in him. I watched my husband come home at night and for the most part sleep well because he knew he did right by his clients. And, those times that he didn't, it was usually because of a down market and he was worried about disappointing them. I can't thank him enough for the life he has given me, both financially and emotionally. It is very nice to like, admire, laugh with, and love the person you are spending your life with. Just a point to be made for future generations.

CHAPTER 18
JACK AND CHARISE

Jack and I were "introduced" by mutual friends. Wilma and Ed Gasson used to live next door to Jack and Marcie in San Ramon. Their daughter, Lea, was a good friend of mine. Both Wilma and Lea thought we would be perfect for each other. And, so after hearing about Jack McHugh over and over again, I decided to call him. I called him one Sunday night and told him who I was. He had also heard about me from Wilma. After I introduced myself, I sort of stumbled, and then said, "Ok, here's the thing. I've never called a man before. I don't know what to do next?" Jack said, "Well, you could start by asking if I want to go for a drink sometime?" He coached me through the entire phone call. At the end, we decided to meet for a drink at the Custom's House where I worked as the Banquet Director. We hit it off great over cocktails, and I walked him out to parking lot. I described earlier how when we walked to his car, he put on a baseball cap and jumped in his Renegade Jeep in a three-piece suit. City and country, all in one man. If it wasn't love at first sight, it was certainly, intrigue at first sight!

Jack and Charise, Banff, Canada 1984

After Jack and I met at The Customs House for the drink, he invited me out to dinner. We both happened to be skiing with our boys at Northstar (Lake Tahoe) the next weekend, so we met up there. I was staying with friends in Incline, so we actually didn't go to dinner, but spent Saturday and Sunday skiing together. On Sunday, I drove to his condo in Northstar so we could follow each other back at least until we had to split and go in different directions. Jack lived in Sausalito, and I, in Foster City. He later told one of his friends that I was geographically undesirable, but very worth it. At his Northstar condo, he kept trying to kiss me, but Byron or Josh kept interrupting us. We finally had our first kiss in the kitchen, and to this day, if you ask him what I was wearing he can tell you, a red sweater.

A couple of months later he arrived at my house late at night, unexpectedly, after Opening Day on The Bay. I got a phone call from Susie, my best friend. He didn't know who it was calling, and to give me privacy, he went outside. I lived on a canal and had a row boat on my dock. He knew his good friend, Bruce, lived right near me, so he decided to take the row boat and see if he could find him. As he was paddling down the canal, wearing only a black towel around his waist, the boat started taking on water. He sees Bruce in his bathrobe through Bruce's sliding glass door, pulls in, gets out and knocks on the door. The towel is soaking wet so he leaves it in the boat. What are the chances of all the canals in Foster City, that Bruce and I live on the same one? Bruce opens the door and says, "Nice to see you Jack!" He looks down and says, "Looks like you need a towel!" As if this is an everyday occurrence to see a naked man at your back door. Bruce gives him a robe, calls his wife, Nanette, down, and then Jack calls me and describes where Bruce lives on the other side of the canal. In my nightgown and robe, I must drive his Jeep, since his car is blocking mine in the garage. I go jerking down the road, driving a stick shift I have never driven, and find their house. Here we are, all in bathrobes on a Sunday evening, at 11:00 at night, having wine with their Scottie dog doing the unmentionable to a stuffed toy on the floor. This is suburbia? I'm thinking, oh my, life with this man is going to be interesting! Finally, they say, "Well, so nice of you to drop by, and for dressing up, Jack". And, I say, "Well, didn't the invitation say Black Towel?"

Wedding photo in Lucille's wedding dress

As I thought, Jack loved the Ranch. He often wore Western clothing, cowboy boots and hat, and he fit right in with the locals and the town. I was thrilled. We soon ousted the tenant we had at the time and took the Ranch back over. All the sisters were at a point where their kids were old enough to enjoy it, Valerie had moved back to California from Colorado, and it was, as always, a joint decision. Jack did a lot of the outside cutting and burning, and Johnny and Dobie were busy re-paneling the walls and ceilings of the main house. All our times, over the years at the Ranch, have been happy ones and later, I would even keep our horses there.

1984 Jack, Josh, Charise, Tamara at our Reception

Us with The Groves Family- Jody, Peter, Rosie, and Greg

Jack and I were married January 14, 1984 at our friend's house in Corte Madera on a Saturday. Jack told his mother he was going to ask me to marry him, and Mombo immediately said, "Jack are you sure? She's such a nice girl!" Jack said, "Ma, you're my mother!" It was pretty funny. Jack then came home late Wednesday night and got down on his knee and asked me, "Will you marry me?". No ring, he wasn't that well prepared. I said, "What, you want to run that by me again?" He said, "You really make a guy feel comfortable, Charise." I said, "When?" Jack goes and gets the calendar off the laundry room wall and says, "How about Saturday?" I said, "You really needed a calendar for that one, Jack." And, so we were married at Peter and Rosie Groves home in Corte Madera, with Byron walking me down the aisle, Tamara as my Maid of Honor, and Joshua as

Jack's Best Man. I wore my mother's purple wedding dress from 1938 and her wedding ring. Jack would buy a beautiful ring and diamond for me later, in time for our March reception. We spent our wedding night in the Groves Volkswagen bus decorated very nicely by Tamara and the Groves daughter, Jody. Then Monday we flew off to Canada and took the Via train from Vancouver to Banff.

Everyone on the train knew we were on our honeymoon, since Jack left the champagne in his luggage and made the porter go get it. The train was filled with pastors, ministers and priests going to a Pastoral Convention. When I finally emerged from our cabin to the dining car at noon the next day, I got a standing ovation. Banff was incredible, even at 16 degrees below zero. We had a sleigh ride, we skied at two resorts, and stayed in the old Banff Hotel in the honeymoon suite.

When we met, the kids were 3, 4, and 5. The combining of the families went well and the kids all got along and grew up as siblings. We moved into Ocean Colony in Half Moon Bay before we got married to make sure this would work. It did.

One Sunday, we came home from skiing at Northstar, Tahoe, and I had torn my ACL on my knee while skiing. Jack decided he would make dinner. An odd decision, since Jack doesn't cook. And, I mean, didn't know how to make hard boiled eggs when I met him. A peanut butter and jelly sandwich was about all he could handle. He told me he was going to make scrambled eggs. I told the kids, be generous, don't complain, he's trying to help me out. He brought dinner to the family room where I was propped up on pillows. I took one bite, and said, "Uh, Jack, what did you put in the scrambled eggs?" He said, "Well, I've seen you put milk in them, but we didn't have any, but there was some Irish Bailey's Cream on the refrigerator door!" Only an Irishman that has never cooked would think of that substitution. It was awful, it curdled the eggs! Disgusting! Highly, not recommended.

CHAPTER 19
TRAVELING WITH JACK

Charise and Jack
Bristol, England

In September of 1984, Jack and I took a six-week trip to Europe with my father and Camilla Wolfe. Camilla was the wife of a Bohemian friend of dads who had passed away. She was friends with my mother, so Camilla and dad took a couple of trips together (separate rooms), because it gave my dad a companion with similar interests. She was of Mexican decent and had the most beautiful skin imaginable. She also, had an Operatic voice and often sang along with the musicians at the restaurants where we were dining. The Broadway hit musical, "Cats" had been released on Broadway that year and "Memories" had become a hit song. I don't think any of us ever heard it sung better than Camilla's rendition.

Charise, Marshal, Camilla Wolfe

On the plane to Europe, the movie "Tarzan, the Legend of Greystoke" was playing. You may remember the scene where Tarzan first makes love to Jane. They are in the manor house of Greystoke, and after their coupling, Tarzan reverts to his primal upbringing. He starts jumping around, arms hanging down, making apes sounds, and jumps on the bed on all fours. As I watched it on the plane, somehow, I knew this scene was going to come back to haunt me. Sure enough, we check into our beautiful hotel room, filled with gorgeous antiques and a four-poster bed, the Hotel de Crillon on the Plac de Concorde. My first time in Paris since I was eight, with the love of my life, and I arrange myself on the four-poster bed in a beautiful white peignoir gown. Jack comes out of the bathroom and starts in on his Tarzan impression; scratching under his arms, jumping up on the bed on all fours, making grunting ape sounds. "Whoo, whoo, whoo, ahh, ahh, ahh!" I couldn't stop laughing.

We went to England, France, Austria, Czechoslovakia, and Holland. While in Paris, after dinner one evening, Dad was tired and retired to the Hotel de Crillon. Jack had to go back to the hotel, as well, to call his office due to the time difference. Camilla and I wanted to go to Maxim's around the corner. We told Jack we would meet him there. Upon entering the restaurant Camilla and I asked for a table. We were told, nicely, that we could not be seated unescorted. We told the gentleman that my husband was coming right along, but the waiter said we had to wait. Quite bristly, I might add. I was a little put off by this treatment, but Camilla suddenly got a big grin on her face. She said, "They think we're hookers!" I said, "What?" She started laughing and saying, "Wait until I get home and tell the Bridge ladies that at the age of 69, I was mistaken for a Lady of the Evening!" It made her night. Sure enough, when Jack came, we were seated and treated very well. Up until that time we were persona non-grata for sure.

Marshal and Jack 1984, Paris France

It was hard leaving the kids for six weeks, but they were in good hands with Marcie and Bud, and this was a wonderful opportunity to spend time with my father. At the beginning of the trip we traveled through the English countryside and stayed in Buckland Manor in the Cotswold's. Upon arriving we had tea, and I spotted some horseback riders pulling up to the hotel. Without saying a word to the others, I ran outside and discovered you could rent the horses for a ride. I ordered two horses for the next afternoon. When I came to tell Jack about it, all excited, Dad, at 82, said, "Oh, go order another one for me!" If looks could kill, I would be no more. Jack would not talk to me all night. Finally, I got out of him that he had never been on a horse. He loved Montana, he wore Western clothing, it never occurred to me that he had never ridden. It was a frosty night in a beautiful canopy bed that evidently couldn't get big enough for him.

Hotel Crillon, Paris, France

The next afternoon, I go out ahead and explain to the guide that Jack has never ridden, so what horse can he give him. "Paddy will be good," he exclaims. Perfect! The three of us set off with our guide, and Jack will barely talk to me. I'm trying to teach him how to hold the reins, heel down, toe out, etc. Finally, I ride up to dad and

say, "Dad, if you ever want your daughter to have sex again, you'll go back there and teach my husband how to ride." He did. His first instruction? "Grab your balls and pull them up." Ok, who knew? That wasn't in my wheel house. It came in handy later when I was teaching the boys to ride! I rode off up the hills and back again after the guide was confident with my horsemanship. The countryside was exquisite. Right out of a book, goats climbing on rocks and buildings, lush green meadows, white stucco and thatched cottages. Picture book perfect. It was a long ride. Finally, we got to Snow's End, a quaint little village, with narrow streets. I'm in front of dad, and he suddenly says, "Where's Jack?" I turn around and he is nowhere to be seen. So, I turn my horse around and go to look for him. I find him about a half block back, around a corner, inside a pub. Let me rephrase that, he and the horse are inside a pub. He says, "Where's the reverse on this thing?" I show him how to lower his hands and

Jack and Charise setting out for the ride, Stratford-upon-Avon, 1984

back the horse out of the pub. Dad, now behind me says, "Well, where would you expect to find an Irishman on an Irish horse? In a pub, of course!" We were all so sore the next day we could barely walk. The ride was five hours. However, my husband was speaking to me again, and, for the most part had enjoyed his maiden voyage on horseback.

We had so many fun times with Dad and Camilla on this trip. Dad was a smoker and would light up after dinner. Jack was determined to steal an ashtray from his favorite restaurants. By the way, my mother was the only tourist in the world, probably, that would go to the manager and ask to purchase an ashtray that she wanted. Jack was not doing that. So, one night at the Schwarzenberg Palace in Vienna, when our after-dinner coffee was served, my father looked all over the table for the ashtray, and when not finding one, leaned across the table and flicked his ashes in Jack's sport coat breast pocket, and, sure enough that was exactly where the ash tray was stowed.

Part of our trip, we were following Napoleon Bonaparte's battles, so we went to Czechoslovakia. Once again, I experienced the drab, no color, oppressive feeling of an Eastern block country. Jack had never been behind the Iron Curtain before. We were in a

Jack and Jack Mendel, our guide and driver. Here at Stone Hedge when you could still walk right up to it.

two-week-old stretch Mercedes limousine. Our guide, Franz, who brought us from Austria, told us that he would put a Western newspaper on the dash of the car. The guard would ask if he was finished with it and Franz would say yes. That was how they got to read Western news. It still didn't stop them from putting the mirror under the car, etc. I guess, in some regards, it smoothed our way. You were not allowed to take any Western currency into Czechoslovakia. As we left the Check Point Charlie and drove through the streets, anyone that was on the streets turned their back to us. We were in a Mercedes Limo. They thought we were Russians.

Jack, Charise, Dee Bauer, Marshal, 1984

Our Hotel Inter-Continental was decorated right out of the 1960s; turquoise naugahyde sofas, chunky amber glass, elevators still run by an operator, and red metal doors on the hotel rooms. The rooms were long and narrow and bed, dresser, desk were all built-ins like in a dormitory. I told Jack and my Dad, I thought they must have come to the US to learn about hotels and never got off the train. There were televisions, but nothing aired accept World War II news clips showing Russian tanks going into Poland, or France conquering the cities. It was nothing but propaganda, and frankly, scary!

Trude Schwartz, Charise, Hellmut Schwartz, Camilla, 1984

Prague was gorgeous, the bridges with their gold accents, the citadel on the hill. Jack bought a Russian army jacket, and I had a green cap with a red star on it that someone had given me from China that he borrowed. He would walk across the Liberty Bridge, his arm outstretched, saluting saying, "Comrades, Comrades!" I wanted to kill him. I told him, "Let me be clear. When that plane takes off for Amsterdam, I will be on it, even if you are in jail. You can't kid around like this!" We made it out ok, and I wanted to kiss the Dutch ground upon arriving! Prankster!

While in Vienna, I kept calculating the price of things from schillings to dollars very fast. Finally, my father said, "Ok, Charise, we know that you are not as good at math as Jack or me, so how are you converting the 5.2% ratio of schilling to the dollar so fast?" I said, "Oh, it's 5.2%? Yeah, you're right I can't calculate that fast, but if you slash off the last number and divide by two you are really close and only a few dollars off by the time you get to $100!" They just looked at me, and then each other, and burst out laughing. Hey, where there's a will, there's a way!

One other funny story that happened in Vienna. Jack wanted mouthwash. We went to a Farmacia. No one spoke English, had no idea what he was looking for. So, I started pantomiming; unscrewing the top off a bottle, taking a swig, swishing it around in my mouth, making gargling sounds, and finally spitting it into an imaginary sink. They understood perfectly and got him the mouthwash. On the way out of the store, I said, "It's a good thing I didn't need Tampons." Jack said, "Oh, Charise, that's terrible! You have such a warped sense of humor sometimes." I shrugged my shoulders, went up the street to where my father had the door open to the back seat of the car, feet on the curb, smoking a cigarette. I explained my pantomiming, and he said, "Wow, I guess it was a good thing he didn't need a suppository!" I said, "Go ahead, Jack, tell

Dee, Marshal, Jack, 1984

my father he's got a warped sense of humor, because obviously, the apple doesn't fall far from the tree!"

Helmut Schwartz had been our guide through Germany and Austria when I was a child. We landed in Vienna just to see him for our Middle East trip when I was twelve. He came to the United States often and visited my parents. He also visited Jack and me at Tahoe one New Years. He was a guide in his younger years and then became an engineer. He was, also, a train buff and had a train going through his house about 12 inches from the ceiling on shelving. It went from one room to another, even the bathroom. At 5pm sharp, no matter what you were doing, the train pulled out of the station and traveled around the house through every room. It was magnificent! And, very entertaining! So, on this trip we visited his house again. Not the same one, a new one. Here the trains were relegated to a very large room downstairs. But, no museum has a more complete exhibit as Helmut did.

It was a fabulous trip and before leaving London, Princess Diana gave birth to Prince Harry. They are some of my fondest memories I have with my father.

In 1984, my dad took us to Los Angeles to the Olympic Games. We met Dee Bauer there, a friend of my parents from Texas. Dee was always a lot of fun. We took a trip to Las Vegas with her and Valerie and Dobie a couple of years later. She had a great sense of humor. In Los Angeles, Dad rented a limousine because, at 82, he could no longer do the long walks. The limo would drop us off right by the stadium or venue we were going to watch. Jack had an ABC News baseball cap that he loaned to dad for the sun. We soon realized that getting out of a long black limousine, everyone thought Dad was an ABC executive, so, we got further VIP treatment. We saw swimming, diving, and a lot of track and field, of course, my dad's first choice. It was a great time.

In 1985, we took a trip on the Orient Express from London to Venice with John and Terry Helm. You take the train from London to Folkston, then a ferry across the

Charise and Jack boarding the Orient Express, 1985

English Channel (and yes, it is as rough as you have heard), then you board the train again and travel overnight to Venice. The cocktail car is complete with a grand piano and a pianist that stays up until 3am, or at least that is when he finally asked us if he could go to bed. The wood work in the staterooms, the halls, and entertainment cars are inlaid with designs of geometric shapes, flowers, and scenes. The food is to die for. Each course is a master piece of presentation. We were on the train with a prince and princess from South Africa. She was a doctor, and he was a stock broker on Wall Street. Also, aboard were couples from England, Australia, New York, New Orleans, and Cleveland. Dinner was a black-tie affair and all the women dressed in 1920's attire, complete with boas and headbands.

We ended the train trip in Venice, spent a few nights, and then Jack and I went to our favorite European city (village), Portofino. We have been several times, and we just love it. We rent a row boat from Papa, and buy cheese, fruit, and bread from Mama, then row around the point and drop anchor and swim, snorkel, and sunbathe all day. Gloriously relaxing. On one particularly lazy day, as we were laying on the pad of the boat sunbathing, Jack had other ideas. I said, "We can't do that, what if a boat comes?" He said, "We'll hear the engine." A little while later we see something come around the rock out of the corner of our eyes, and immediately we both roll off into the water on opposite sides of the boat. A family of mama, papa, and four bambinos come rowing past us as we wave from the water. When they passed, we burst out laughing, neither one of us thought about a row boat!!

Following Napolean's battles into Czechoslovakia

On one of our trips to Portofino, I wanted a sandwich. I went to the store, bought French bread, prosciutto, Swiss cheese, lettuce, and found some mayonnaise. We went back to the Hotel Nationale right down at the wharf. We ate outside on our ground floor patio, and along came a wharf cat. I fed him some prosciutto and he gobbled it up. We decided to do the same thing the next day because it was so good. This time the wharf cat visited us again, dropping a dead bird at my feet. He sat back as if to say, "Yesterday, you fed me, today, I feed you." I looked at him and sweetly said, "No, that's okay, Kitty, you go ahead." I love it when you can see the wheels turning in an animal's head!

Charise overlooking Portofino, 1985

Charise, Josh, Byron, Tamara, Jack 1987

We took the children to Hawaii Thanksgiving 1987 and had a wonderful time swimming, playing on the beach, snorkeling, dining, seeing a show, and touring Oahu. I wanted them to see the Hawaii I grew up with, but it had already changed a great deal. The old Halekulani had been torn down and replaced with a high rise. We stayed at the Royal Hawaiian because it still had some old Hawaiian charm. I took them to north shore to see a surfing competition, but the waves were too high to show them the rock cave I used to swim though. We did get shaved ice at Haleiwa. Many of my old haunts no longer existed around the island, I hated the new freeway. Stewarts Drug Store with its soda counter was gone, and most of Kalakaua Ave. was a mall. At least the International Market Place was still there, somewhat unchanged, and the kids had fun going to some of the stores I frequented as a kid. You could no longer get a bikini made for you for

Byron, Josh, Charise, Jack, Tamara 1987

$10 flat. The miniature golf had been replaced with a video arcade though so they had fun there. Oh, well, such is progress, I guess. All in all, we had a fabulous time and it was fun for Jack and the kids to get a taste of a big part of my childhood.

We went to Aspen on the train for our tenth anniversary in 1994. It was beautiful going through the Rockies on the train in the snow. Just like on our honeymoon ten years earlier in Canada. It took twenty-one hours, so we spent the night in a cabin, which we love. Sleeping on a train is a great experience if you've never done it. It rocks you to sleep. We loved Aspen with all the great restaurants and shopping. The skiing was terrific. We stayed in this adorable Fireside Inn at the base of the mountain with a fireplace in every room.

John and Mary Helm, Charise, Jack, 1995

On the way back on the train, we experienced our best "small world" story ever. At breakfast, there was an older woman and her daughter who was holding her new born baby. Their food came before we even ordered, and the daughter was having trouble balancing the baby and cutting her French toast. I offered to hold the baby. She said, no that was okay. I whispered to Jack, "What does she think I'm going to do, jump off the train going 80 miles an hour with her baby?" We then started talking to the mother and daughter, it turned out the mother lived in Chicago, but used to live in Foster City, CA. She was moving back with her daughter since her husband had passed away. She didn't like flying, so they were taking the train across the country. It turned

Charise and Jack, Denali Park, Alaska

out we had some mutual friends from Foster City and somehow, she mentioned she lived in Hillsborough before that. I asked her what street and she said Tiptoe Lane. I got this funny look on my face and said, "You're kidding!" The mother said, "Wait a minute, you're Charise Hale." Then, I said, "Yes, I am, but how did you know?" She looked at her daughter and said, "Let her hold the baby." Turned out, I was the young mother's baby sitter when she about seven and I was about fourteen, they lived on nearby Tulip Court. To this day, I've never heard a better "small world" story!

In 1995, we took our favorite cruise of all time, to Alaska on the Holland America Line. Again, we traveled with John Helm, but this time with his new wife, Mary. If you ever have the chance, take this trip and get a room with a balcony, starboard (right) side of the ship. The views are breathtaking and the ice is Caribbean blue. We went to Ketchikan, Sitka, Juno, and Valdez. We took two helicopter rides, the Mendenhall Glacier and a ride to see moose and doll sheep out of Valdez. We then took the train to Anchorage and another train to Fairbanks, passing Mt. McKinley on the way, and then to Denali Park a couple of days later. The river trip in Fairbanks is one of the best tours I have ever experienced; complete with watching Susan Butcher, the Iditarod winner of four out of five consecutive races, practicing with her pups. "Alaska, where men are men, and women win the Iditarod!" Or, at least they used to. It was an exceptional trip with best friends. We are the Godparents to Mary and John Helm's twin boys, Conner and Christopher.

Mary, Conner, Christopher and John Helm

CHAPTER 20

HORSES, DOGS AND CATS

Soon after marrying we got male and female Golden Retrievers. A sister and brother. Their names were Cornflakes and Wheaties, and we already had our cat named Applejacks. The kids were little and cereal names seemed perfect. In

Tamara, Applejacks, Jack, Josh, Wheaties, Cheerios, Charise, Byron, Cornflakes 1987

1987, Jack surprised me with a horse for my thirty-fifth birthday. I named him "Cheerios", an Egyptian Arabian. Beautiful horse with a typical Arab disposition. Sweet as pie, would nuzzle a kitten, and be so gentle, until you got on him. Then, it was a battle of wills. We came to a mutual understanding. I knew he could kill me, and he knew he had never succeeded in throwing me. I had hours and hours of pleasure with this horse. Riding the agricultural fields in the Coastal valleys and on the mountain tops overlooking the ocean.

One funny story was when I was boarding him at Mr. James Stables. They had geese, and the wife of a goose was killed by a bob cat. Geese mate for life, and the male was, shall we say, royally pissed at the loss of his mate. For some reason, the goose decided he hated men. Josh was still young enough to be accepted, but the minute Byron or Jack set foot on the property this goose would lower his head and come aft er them. One January (1989) afternoon Jack was coming to help me clean up my little barn. The goose took one look and off he went, head lowered, running toward Jack's crotch. Jack ran into the barn and grabbed the metal lid off my garbage can and a broom. Armed, he stepped out with the lid shielding his private parts in front, and using the broom like a gladiator sword. He looked like Don Quiote. His sister, Judy, and nephew, Chris, were there. I wish I had captured that on film. We couldn't stop laughing. Unfortunately, it didn't solve the problem and I had to move Cheerios to another stable.

We soon bought Capt. Crunch for the kids and Jack. I taught all four to ride and a few years later moved the horses to the Ranch. We all had great fun on the horses. My sister, Valerie also had a horse, and we relived our childhood riding all over the nearby mountains. The only disappointment was finding fencing where there had previously been none.

Cheerios, Charise Tamara, Wheaties, Byron, Josh, Cornflakes, Jack, Capt. Crunch, c. 1994

Our husbands would rarely ride with us because we thought nothing of cutting barbed wire, riding through, and wiring it back together. We also, thought nothing of forging our own trails. Our famous last words were, "Oh, yeah, I can see light on the other side, we can get through!" And, most of the time, we did. We'd go out in the morning and say we'd be back in a couple of hours, then arrive back four hours later. It's good we never really got into trouble because I'm sure they wouldn't have started looking for us until dusk.

The dogs and cat passed away, and we got a second set of Goldens, Jameson and Harp. The cats were Bailys and Paddy, and later Guinness. The kids were now in their early twenties, so the alcohol names seemed appropriate. The dogs, after three or four, would be referred to as Golden Recliners because no breed does it better. And, now we have Hennessy and Finnegan and a cat named Irish Mist. We stayed with the Irish alcohol theme. The horses have since passed away and I still miss seeing them at the Ranch. Animals bring such joy into your life, but when you lose them it is so incredibly devastating. I still think the trade-off is worth it, all those years of companionship and devotion!

CHAPTER 21

TAHOE, THE FAMILY COMPOUND

We took the children skiing in Tahoe throughout their childhood, renting a friend's Condo in Northstar, north Lake Tahoe area at first. In 1989, we bought a house in Northstar, a cute little A frame with a magnificent view of Martis Valley. Up until that time, Jack had never been to Tahoe in the summer. We had so much fun at the pool, river, lake, and hiking in the mountains. We even took the horses up for two weeks one summer. In 2001, we

Byron, Charise, Jack, Tamara, Josh 1992

purchased a bigger house at the end of Skidder Trail, also in Northstar. It was a magnificent house with an even better view of the valley and Castle Peak. There was a water fall complete with real granite rocks and a bridge leading into the master bedroom. And, the shower was a rock cave with moss growing on the rocks.

Then, in 2005, we moved to a house just outside of Old Greenwood, two miles east of Truckee. It was only two years old on an acre of land. We named it Coyote Ridge. We have been upgrading and adding to it ever since. We love this house and property. It has a 180-degree view of Mount Rose, Martis Peak, Northstar, Squaw Valley, and Castle Peak.

A little bit of interesting trivia. Truckee will often be the coldest spot in the nation on the weather report. Especially during the summer at night. It can be in the 80s during the day and 39 degrees at night. The Truckee River is opposite us and a little east is where "The Ice House" existed. This was a stone building between the river and the railroad tracks. They would pull water out of the river and pour it into blocks that would soon be ice. It would stay frozen all year long due to the stone building, the surrounding ice, and the year round low temperatures at night. They would load the ice onto railway cars, and this serviced the grand hotels of San Francisco during the late 1800s, like the Sheraton Palace.

Coyote Ridge, Truckee, CA

As mentioned, we overlook the train and the Truckee River. And, you don't see a single house. There is a swimming hole at the river and the dogs have the best time! We have all had such fun in the river and at the Old Greenwood pool. We have a family reunion every summer with one branch or another and the kids come for Christmas when they can. The kids can swim in the summer,

Winter view from the backyard of Coyote Ridge

and sled and ski in the winter. The driveway makes a wicked sled run! Santa visited one Christmas Eve and the grandchildren were beside themselves with joy. We love our time in Tahoe and are truly blessed to have both the ocean and the mountains.

Jack and Charise 2018

Jack and I have been blessed to have a good solid marriage with wonderful children, awesome in-law kids, and now six grandchildren between us. I must thank Jack for always balancing his career with his home life. He has worked hard, loves being a financial advisor and helping his clients, and has provided us with a very comfortable life style. But, he has always come home at a reasonable time and had his family life. We've had our ups and downs, every marriage has. Commitment to working it out and an underlining love are the two best ingredients. Let's not

Summer pictures of the view out the back of Coyote Ridge

discount making up!! And, I must include having a sense of humor, that gets you through a lot in life. Don't sweat the small stuff, it's not that important, and certainly not worth harming your marriage over. We are both strong volunteers and share a belief in giving back to our community. It really is true that giving to others is the best gift of all. We hope we leave the world a better place than we found it.

Byron, Charise, Jack, Tamara and Josh, 1992

4th of July at Tahoe, 2016

Left to right: Byron, Sadie, Amy, Annabelle, Chloe, Tamara, Jacob, Charise Jack, Josh, Jaden, Asha, Geri, 2017

Made in the USA
Monee, IL
25 February 2021